PHOTO-HAIKU

Five 五つ
Seven 七つ
Five 五つ

PHOTO HAIKU

Landscapes

Daniel Heller

Word + Image Editions

PHOTO HAIKU: Landscapes

ISBN: 979-8-9990371-0-7
Publisher: Word + Image Editions

The main genre of the book: Photography | Poetry

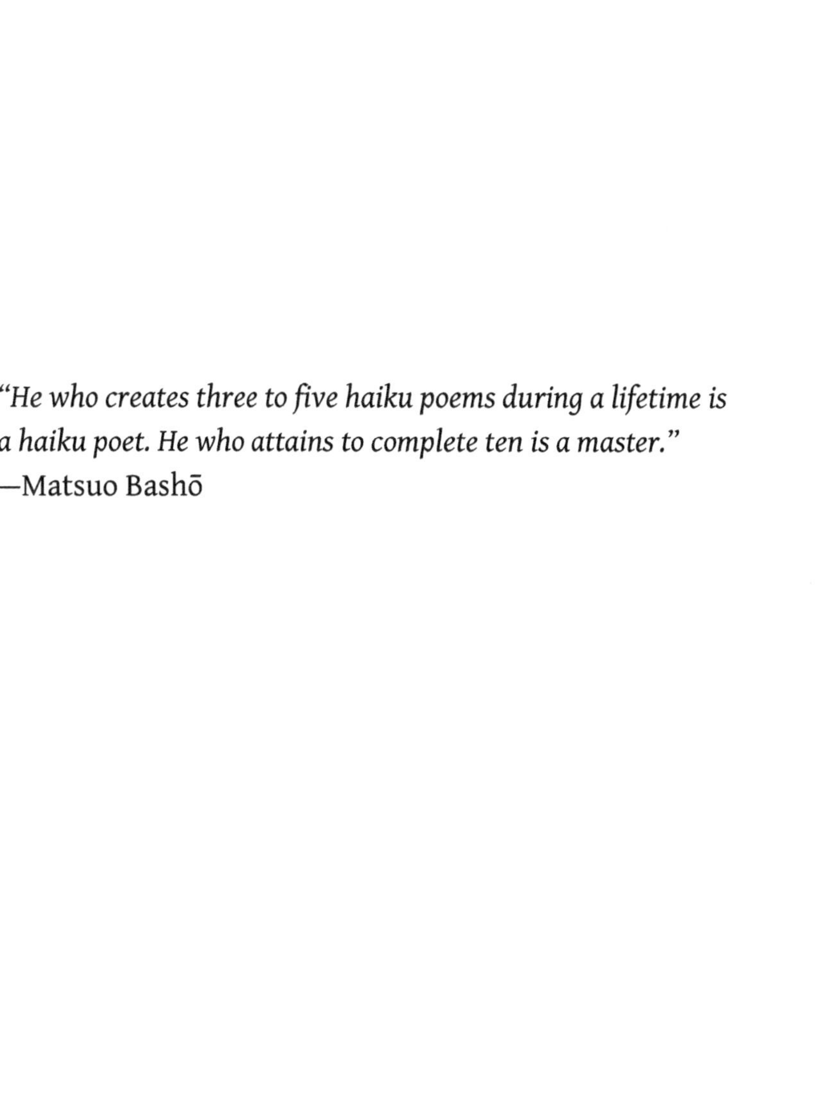

"He who creates three to five haiku poems during a lifetime is a haiku poet. He who attains to complete ten is a master."
—Matsuo Bashō

TABLE OF CONTENTS

PHOTO HAIKU - ILLUSTRATION LIST

THE MOST FAMOUS HAIKU POETS

Basho 1644-1694
Buson 1716-1784
Issa 1763-1827
Shiki 1867-1902

INTRODUCTION

Photo-Haiku, is a relatively new art form. It combines photography with haiku poetry, to present two equally important forms of artistic expression in a symbiotic relationship.

While the photographs included in this book collection were taken some time ago, the haiku poetry was written recently. Significant effort and memory recollection were required to recreate the inspiration associated with each photograph, enabling me to articulate the images through text. Seeing old photographs again evoked old memories facilitating the creation of the haiku. The intent of writing this book and assembling a new collection of artworks, was to recall memory and articulate the poetry inherent in the images.

The old adage, "A picture is worth a thousand words," holds some truth; however, viewers of photographic images often seek to uncover elements of the subjects that the photographs alone cannot fully convey.

To communicate the complete meaning of a visual image without supplementary text is nearly impossible, as interpretation is mostly left to the viewer. A Photograph can elicit multiple interpretations in a viewer's mind, particularly when the viewer lacks context regarding its creation—such as the reason for taking the photograph for example. While a simple text may suffice as a documentary record to convey the meaning, the artistic process requires a much deeper creative process.

In this regard, adding a haiku as an adjunct to an image, introduces an additional dimension of discovery and completes the artistic narrative. Supplementing images with text is a more effective method of conveying meaning and intent, representing a valuable visual artistic endeavor. This was my goal in producing this book.

Throughout this collection, I adhered to the traditional 5-7-5 syllable structure characteristic of the original Japanese haiku. In instances where I deviated, it was due to the necessity of preserving the meaning of the photo as captured.

I hold both photography and haiku in high regard as two similar yet distinct artistic mediums of expression. While they can be presented side by side or overlapping on a page, in this book, the two forms maintain their individual identity and integrity by not encroaching on each other. The haiku accompany the photographs to create a comprehensive experience of the moment —I believe that superimposing text over the image itself would detract from the aesthetic value of the combined presentation.

In keeping with the tradition of Japanese haiku, the thematic focus of the photo-haiku in this book is nature, with a significant emphasis on landscape photography, much of which is inspired by my extensive travels.

It is my hope that the photo-haiku in this collection bring you enduring pleasure and inspiration.

THE NATURE OF HAIKU

What is a haiku? Haiku (俳句) is a very short form of traditional Japanese poetry, a lyric poetic form of artistic expression. It captures a concept, a feeling, or an idea in very few syllables. The simplicity of this form of expression is its beauty. In a haiku a poet transmits to the reader the essence of a particular moment.

In Japanese, a haiku is traditionally printed in a single vertical line, while an English language haiku often appears in three horizontal lines of text. A haiku comprises three lines: five syllables in the first, seven in the second, and five in the last for a total of seventeen syllables.

A well-written haiku poem is usually a juxtaposition of two contrasting parts or ideas with a "cutting word" in Japanese, or punctuation in English. Traditional Japanese haiku focus mainly on nature, including the seasons, weather, landscapes, flowers, trees, grasses, and birds. A haiku is a three-line observation that employs provocative colorful imagery and momentary elucidation. It need not follow the rigid rules of grammatically structured sentences. Any rhyming, punctuation, or capitalization is optional.

The philosophy of haiku is to focus on a brief moment using provocative images to create a sense of sudden enlightenment and illumination. For the most part, the haiku in this book were created by following only some of the traditional criteria listed above.

PHOTO-HAIKU

Similar to a haiku, a photograph is the resulting product of capturing the image of a unique passing moment. To that extent, photo and haiku speak a similar language and can successfully be combined to record the full narrative of an experience.

Photo-Haiku, a fairly new art form, is now a popular creative process. The reason for its success is the fact that photos and haiku are very similar and can be composited easily, because both represent minute portions in time. Haiku expands a photographer's artistic capacity by allowing them to tell viewers in three short lines what they feel at the click of the shutter.

Several techniques exist in which the two sign systems combine. The text may appear adjacent to or on top of the photograph, or it can be separated from the image, as was my preferred method for this book.

WHERE WHAT AND WHEN

The Japanese-American scholar Kenneth Yasuda in his book '*The Japanese Haiku: Its Essential Nature, History, and Possibilities in English, with Selected Examples* (1957).', asserted that to create a successful haiku, three properties must be present in a successful haiku: *where* (place), *what* (object) and *when* (time). According to Yasuda's theory the intent of the haiku is contained in the concept of a "haiku moment," "that moment of absolute intensity when the poet's grasp of his intuition is complete so that the image lives its own life."

This notion of the haiku moment has been defined as "an aesthetic moment" a timeless feeling of enlightened harmony as a poet's nature and environment are unified. The passing momentary experience that comes alive through the precise perception of the image." (Wikipedia).

PHOTO-HAIKU ARTWORKS

NATURE

in dreamy nature
—love is inevitable—
in the spring of life

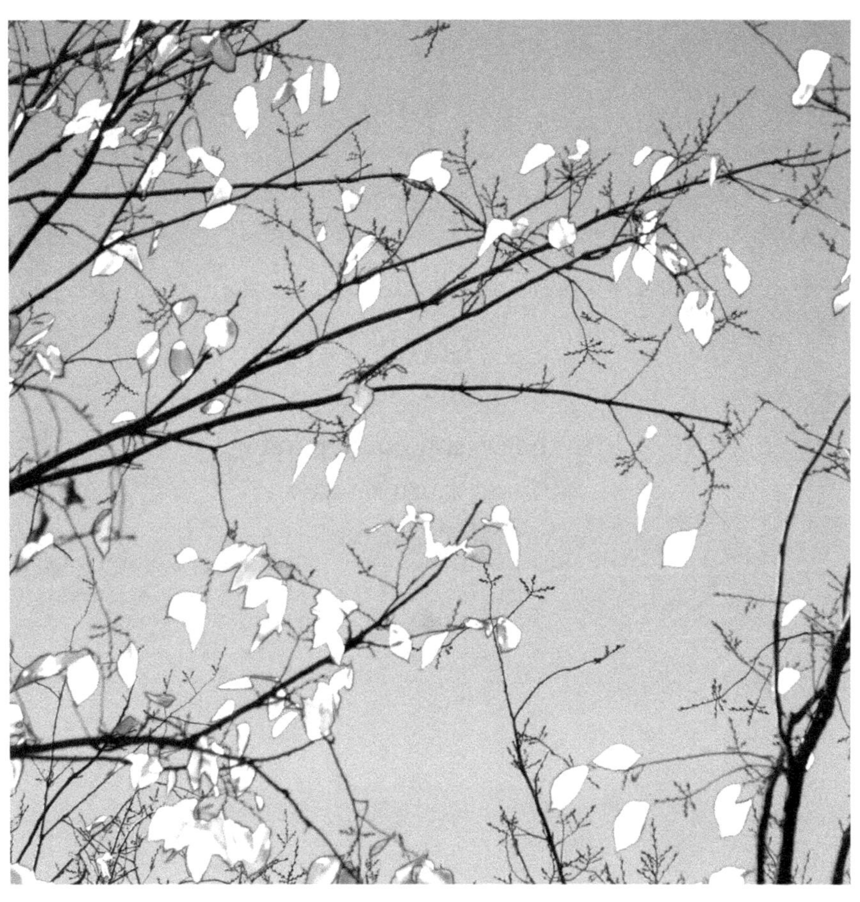

GLOW

in the crystal liquid pond
autumn morning glow
six forty-three

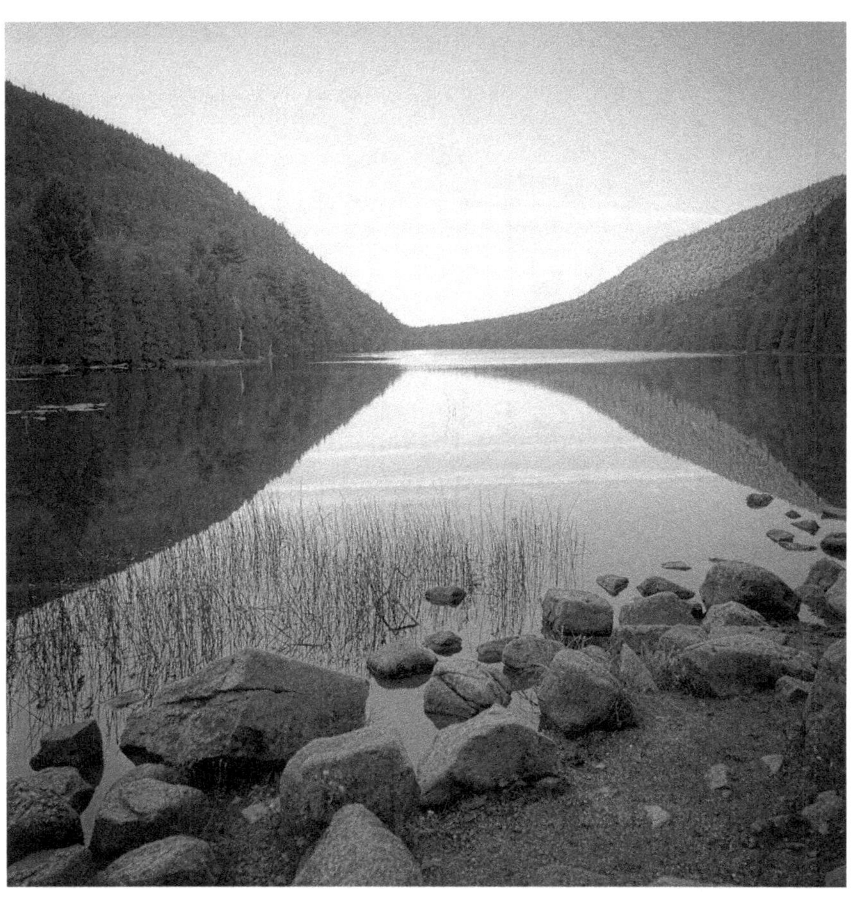

AVIGNON

standing on the famous bridge
birth of day I watch
—dawn I am so young

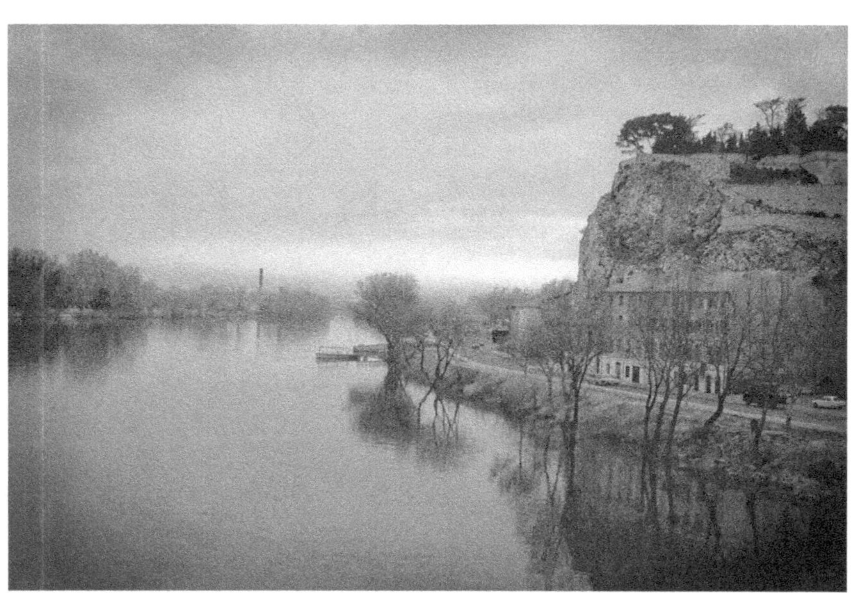

FLANDERS

in the Flanders meadow
sheep graze under clouds
—imminent storm now

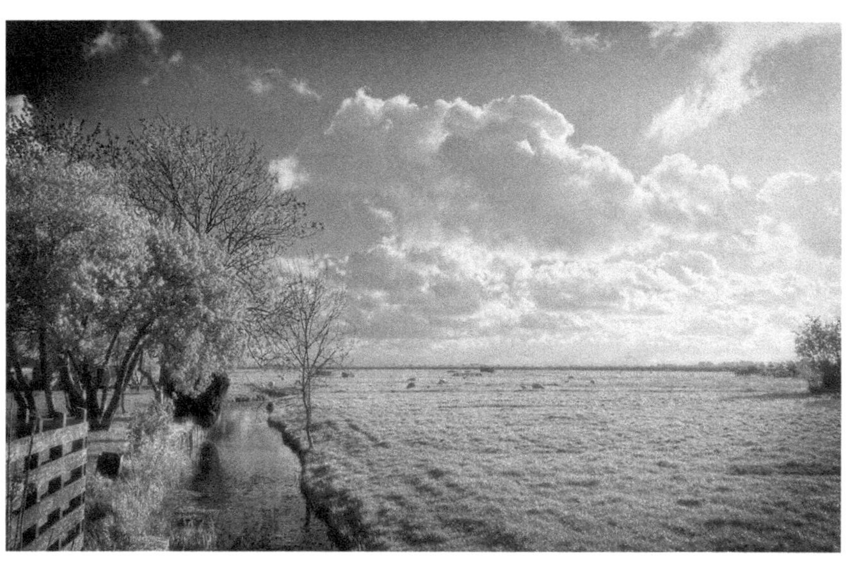

BRIDGE

in the white meadow
a wood bridge is decaying
—winter is coming

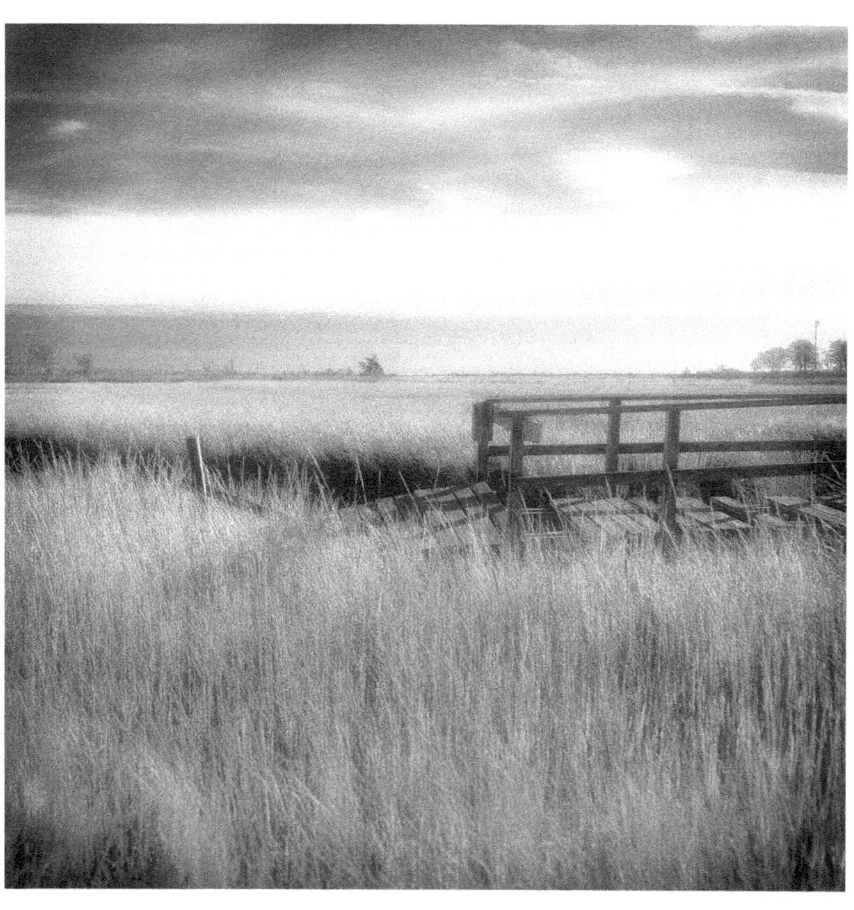

TREE

at the tree
chasing winter clouds
it's good to dream—

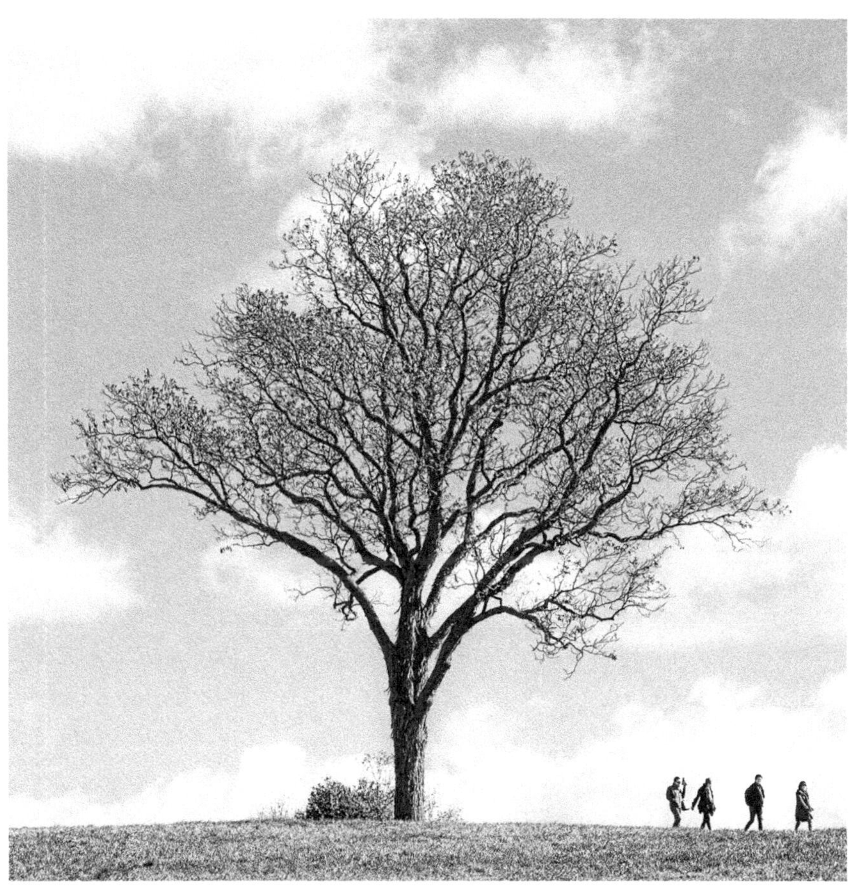

LIGHT

in the deep forest
light and shadows play—
autumn has arrived

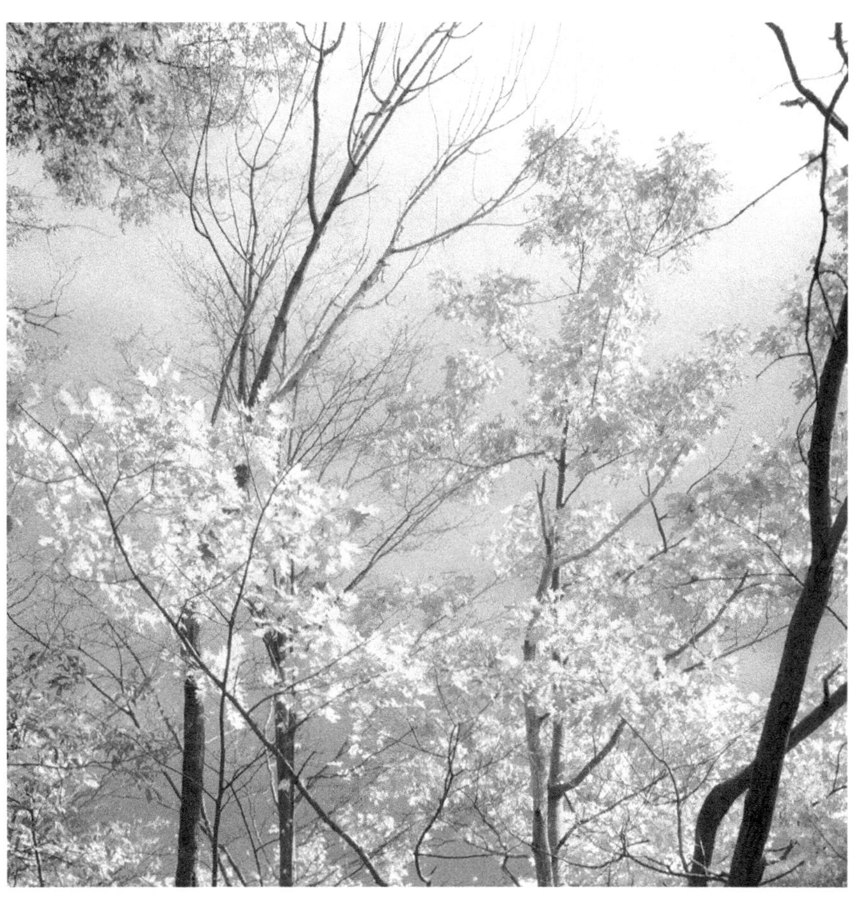

TEXTURE

grasses at the beach
smiling at the passing clouds
the morning texture

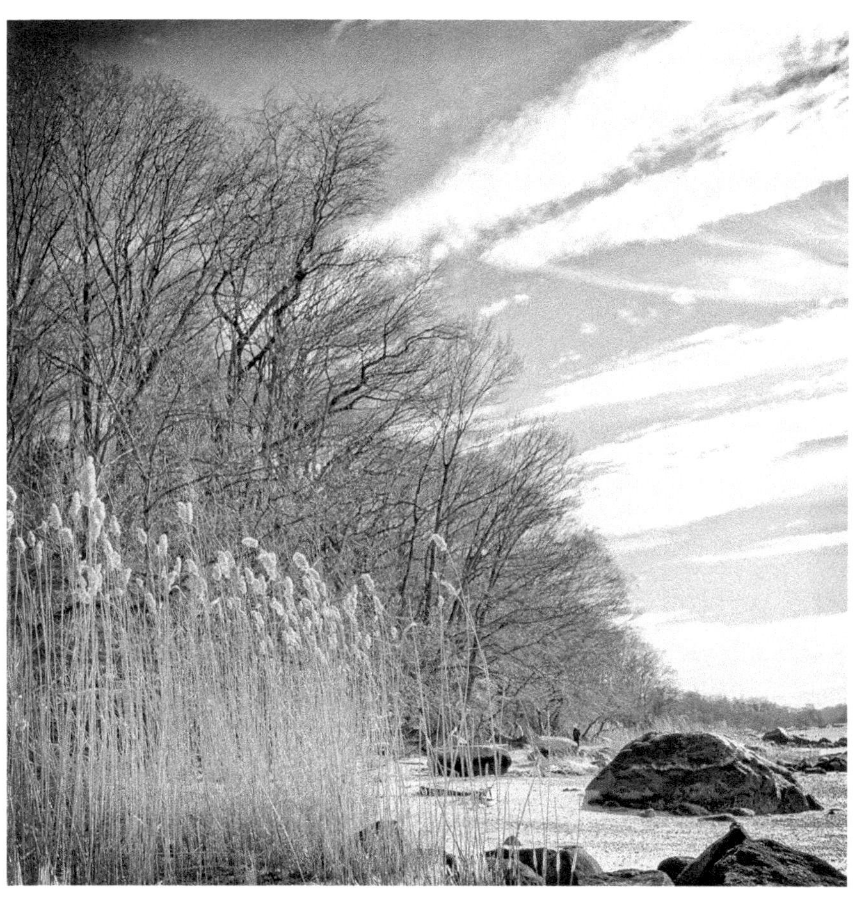

ACADIA

loud sea winds
thrusting waves ashore—
coastal morning

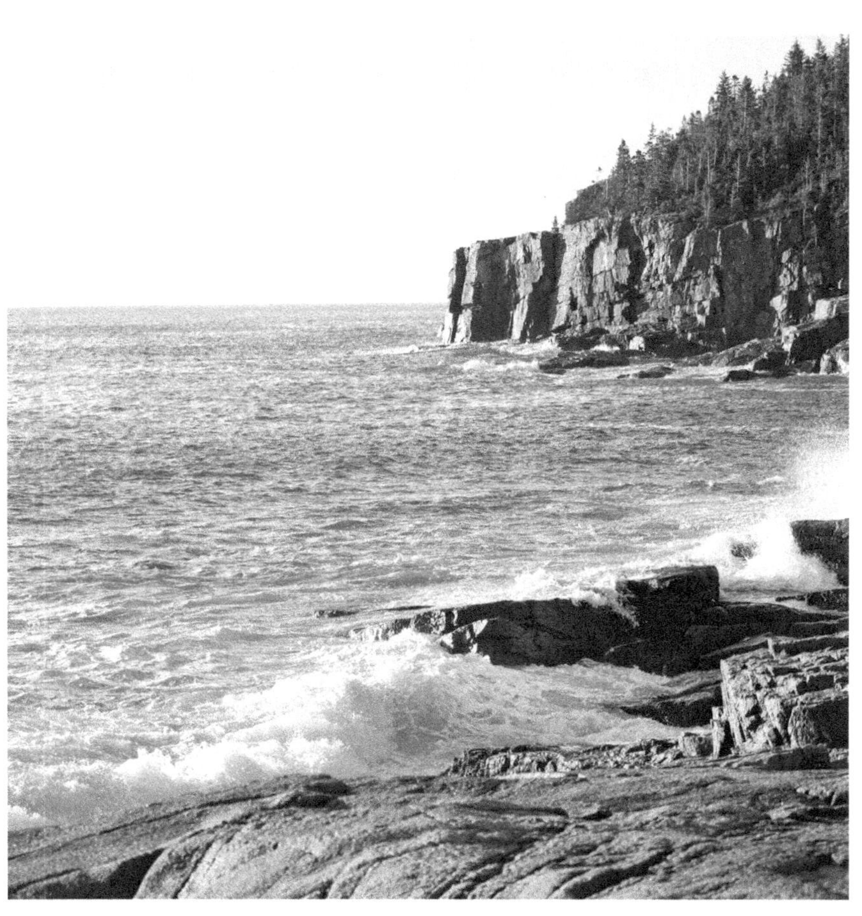

HAIL

in the irish land
hail laden clouds exploding—
early morning walk

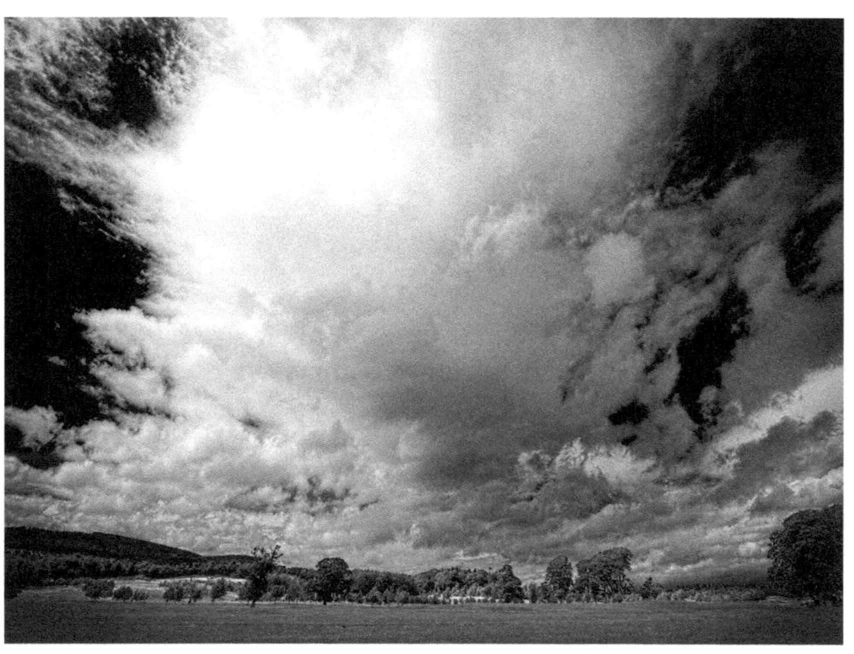

HIDDEN

by the water pond
bridge secluded from view
—autumn season vibes

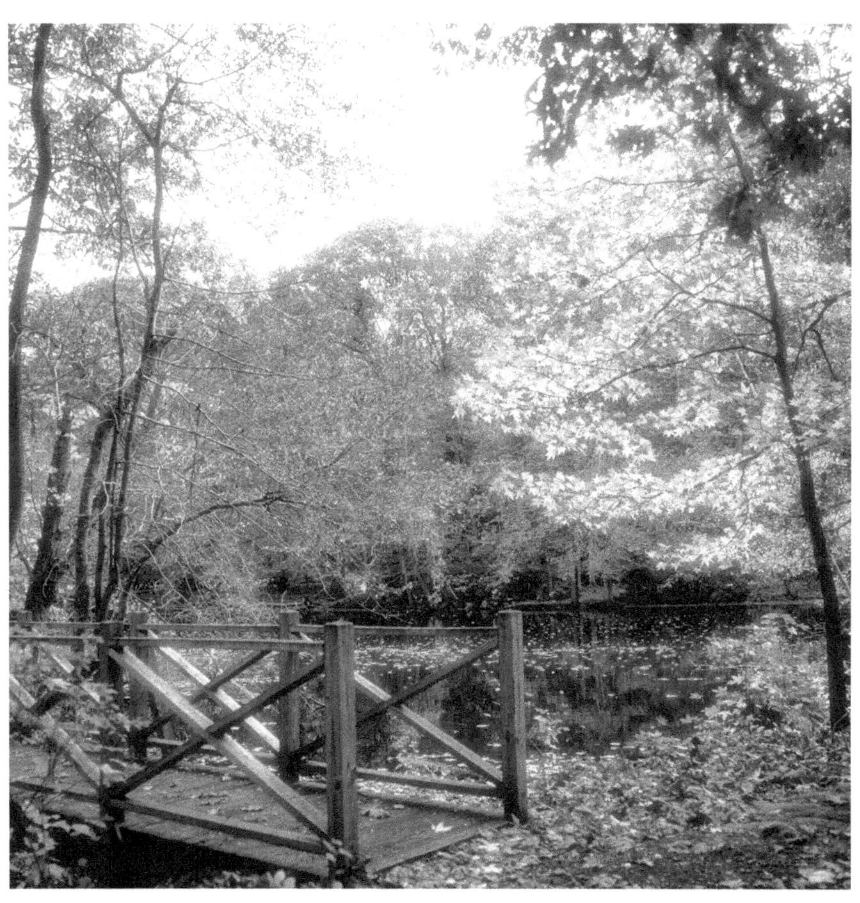

FROZEN

frozen in the lake
dead shadows emerge—
winter has arrived

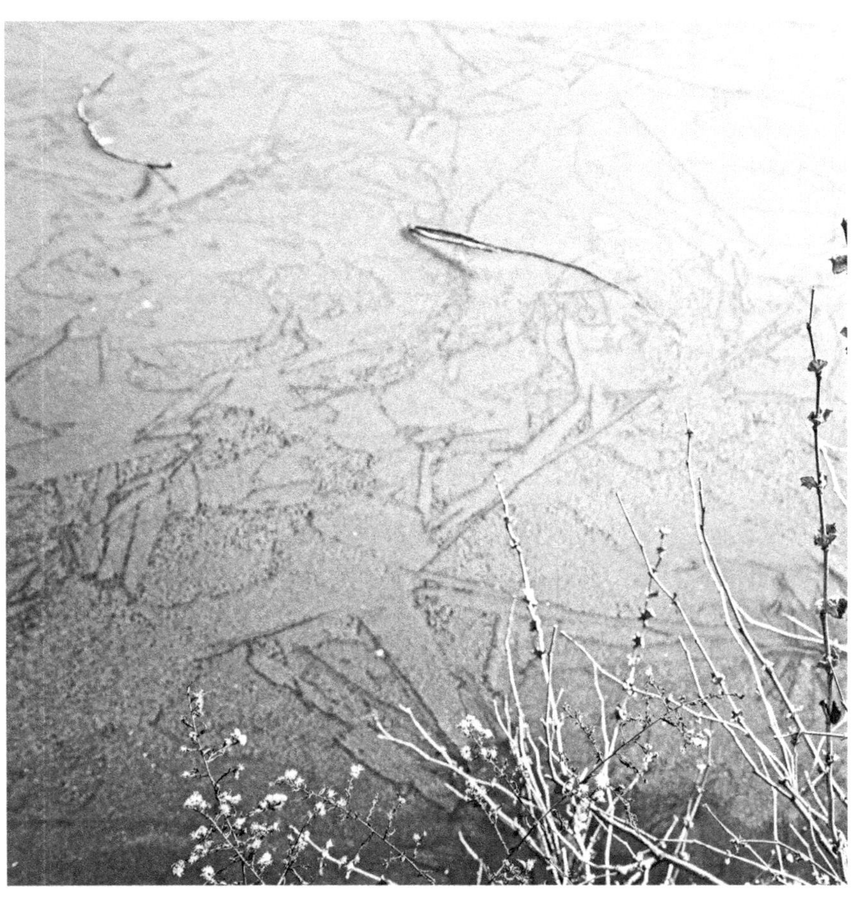

BELVOIR

at belvoir castle
olive grove bathes in the sun
long long time ago

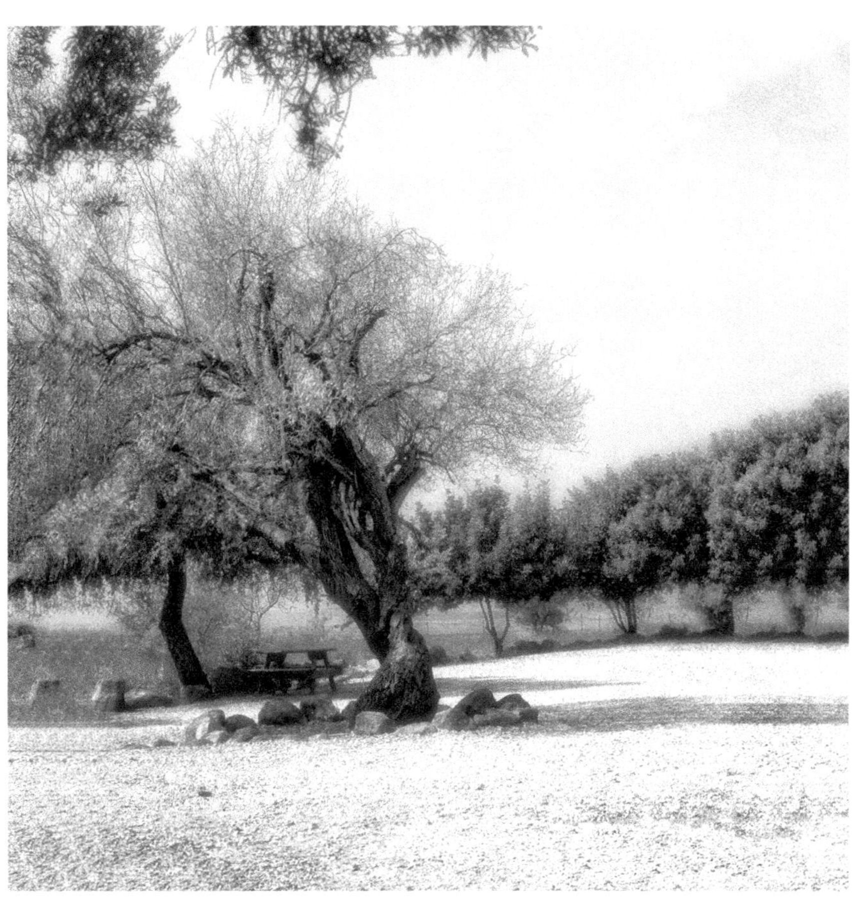

HORIZON

low horizon space
bathing in a morning haze
—beginning of time—

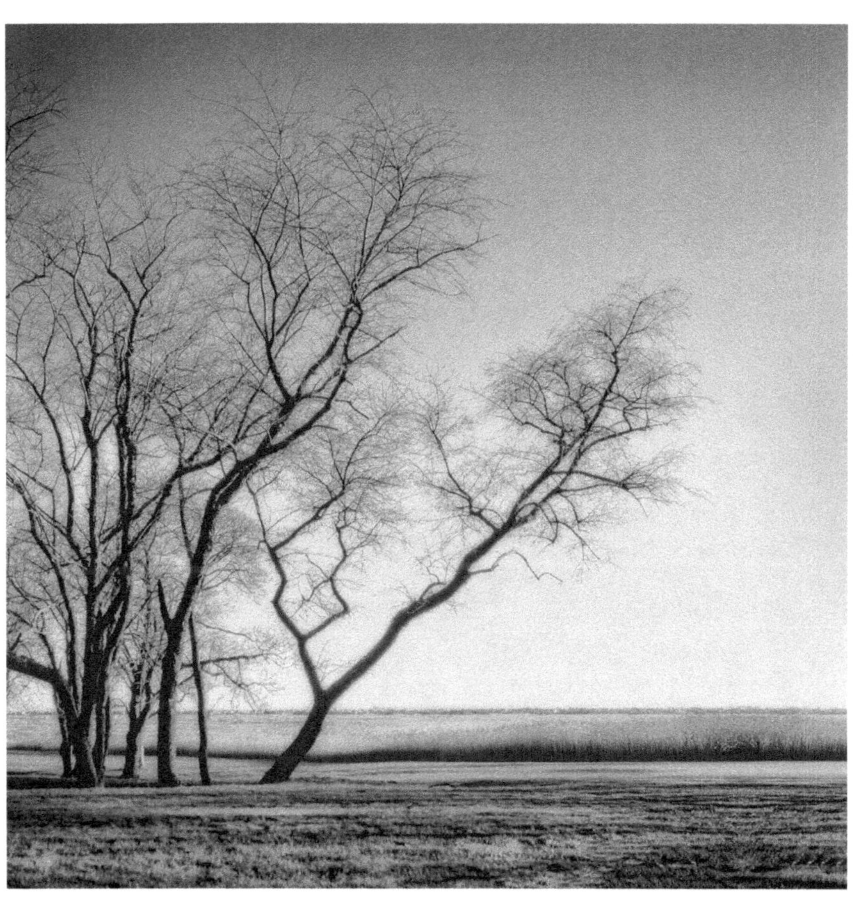

BOAT

at the blue lake dock
boat is ready to sail
last day of summer—

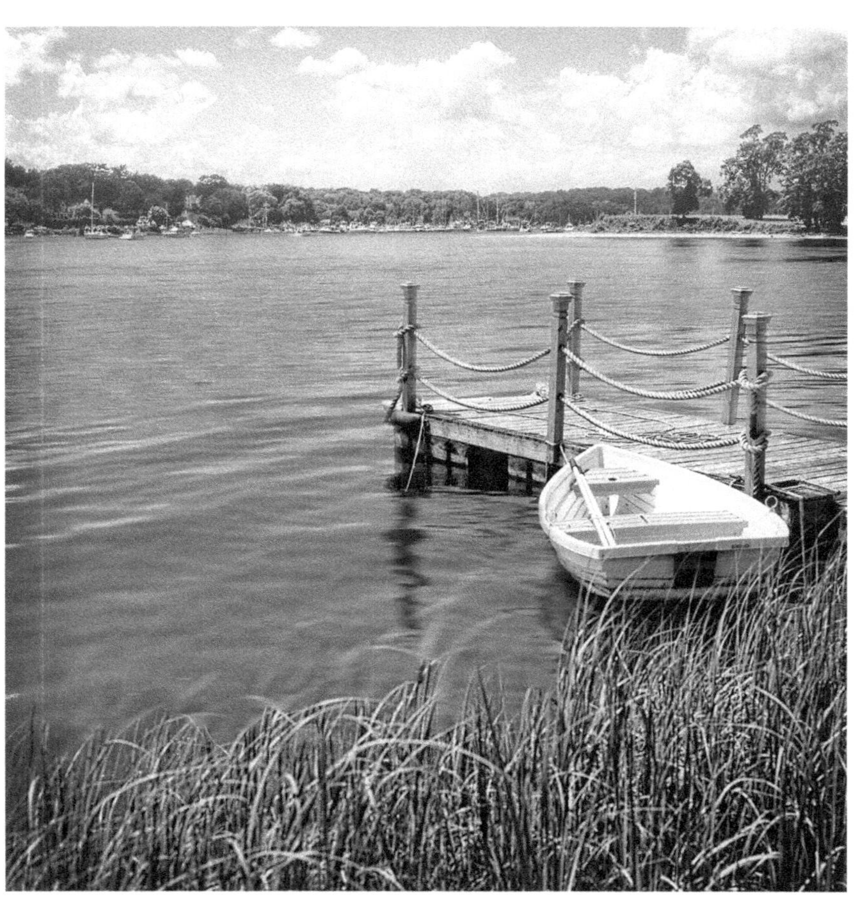

MOHER

atlantic rocks
with brute force
long ago detached

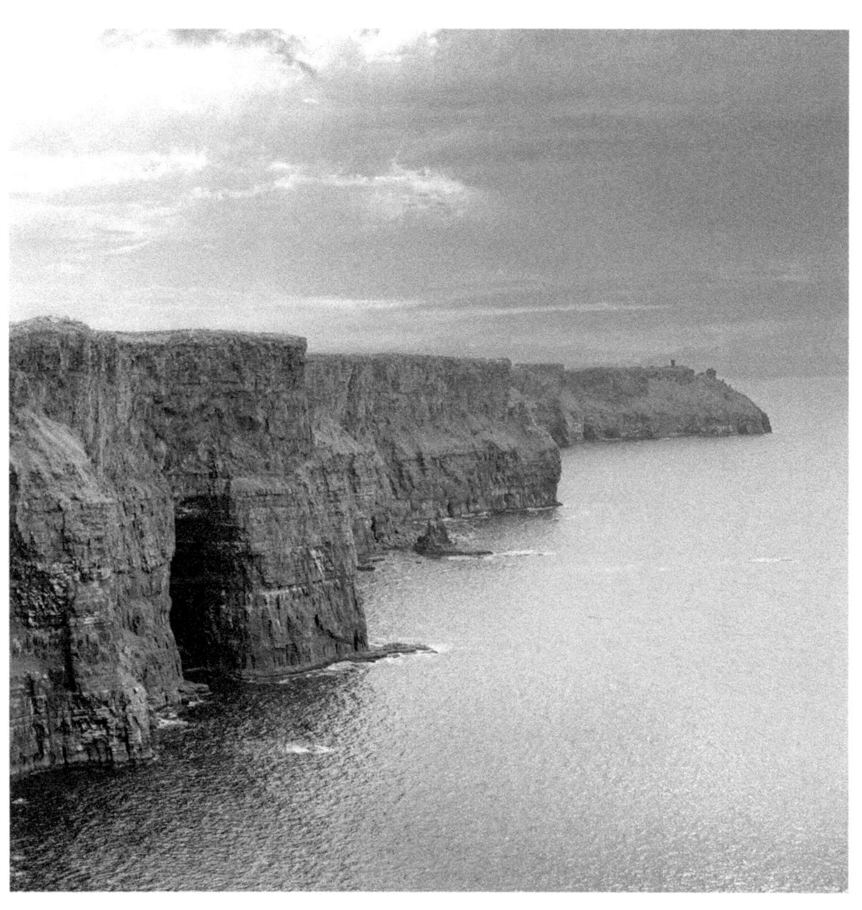

SWAN

at the island lake
swan chasing shadows of light—
boats are leaving soon

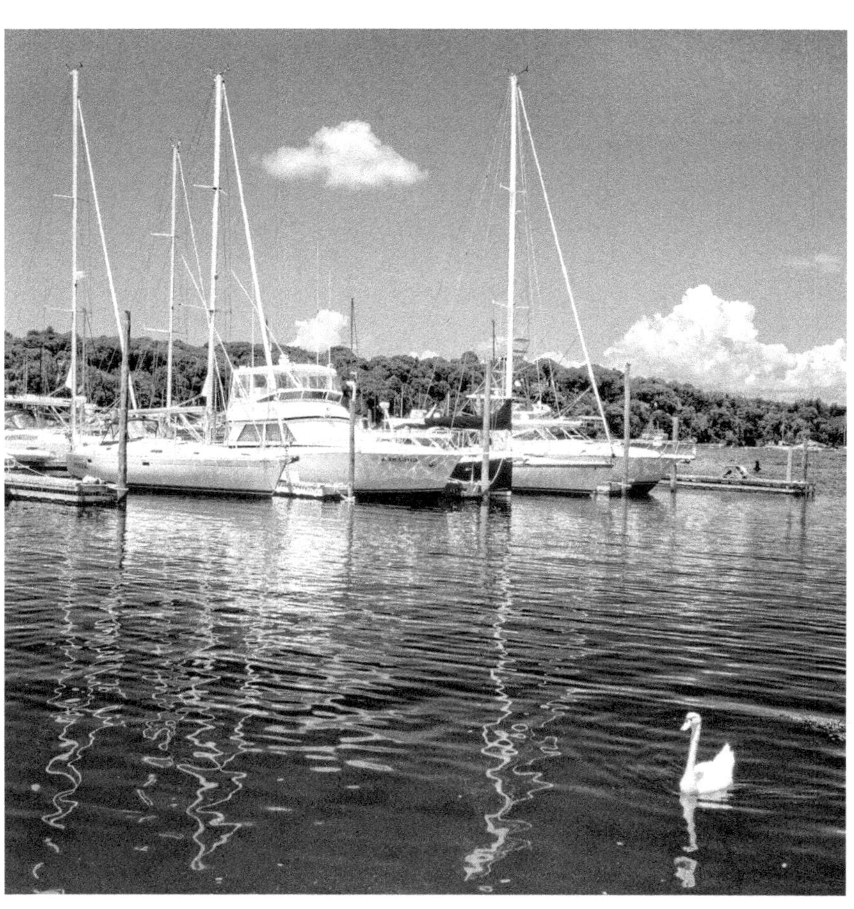

AUTUMN

at the valley pond
trees have already undressed
winter coming now

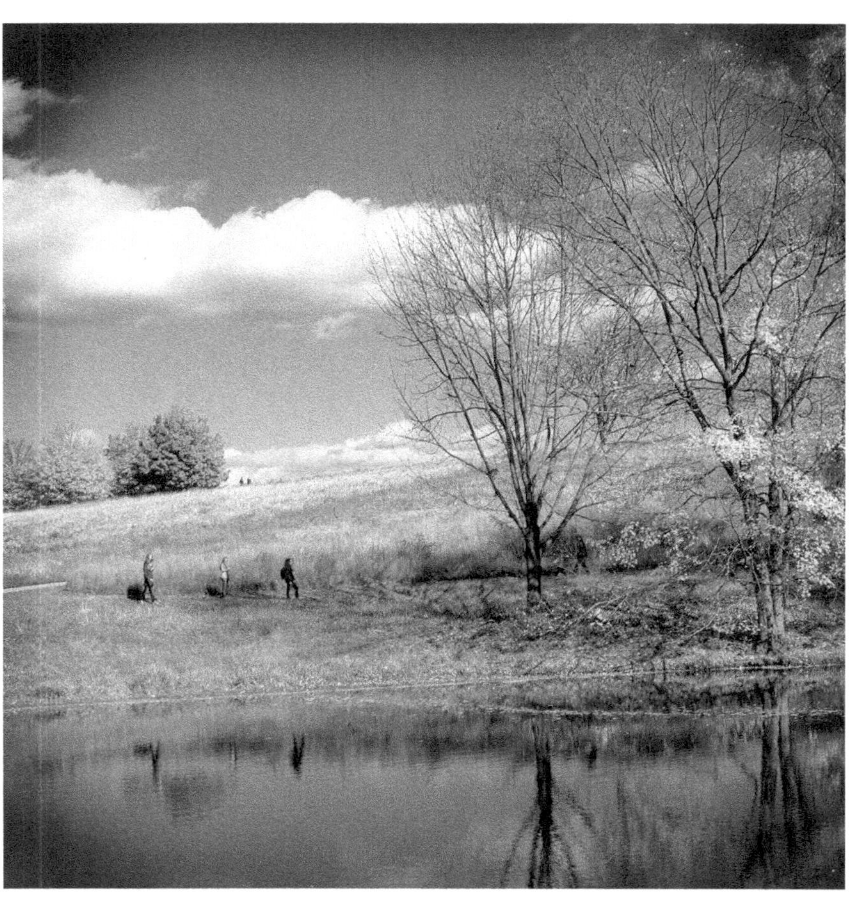

VITALETA

on the hill
private ancient chapel
—spring is magic

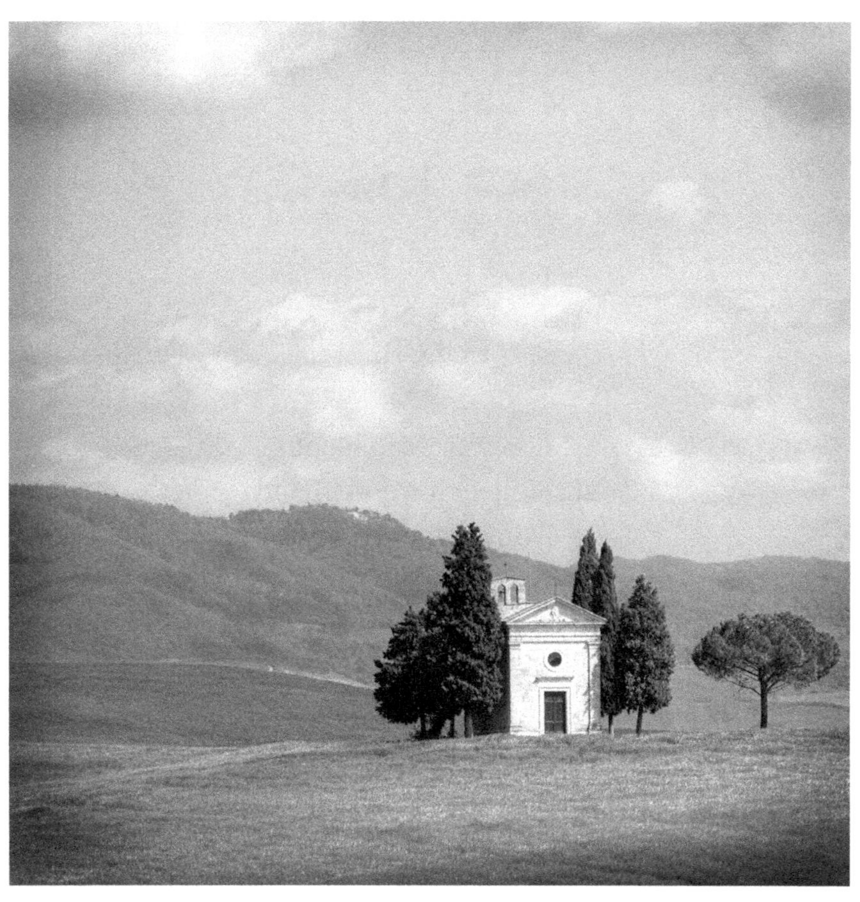

COLORS

colored trees in bloom
at the sleeping quiet pond
—winter approaching

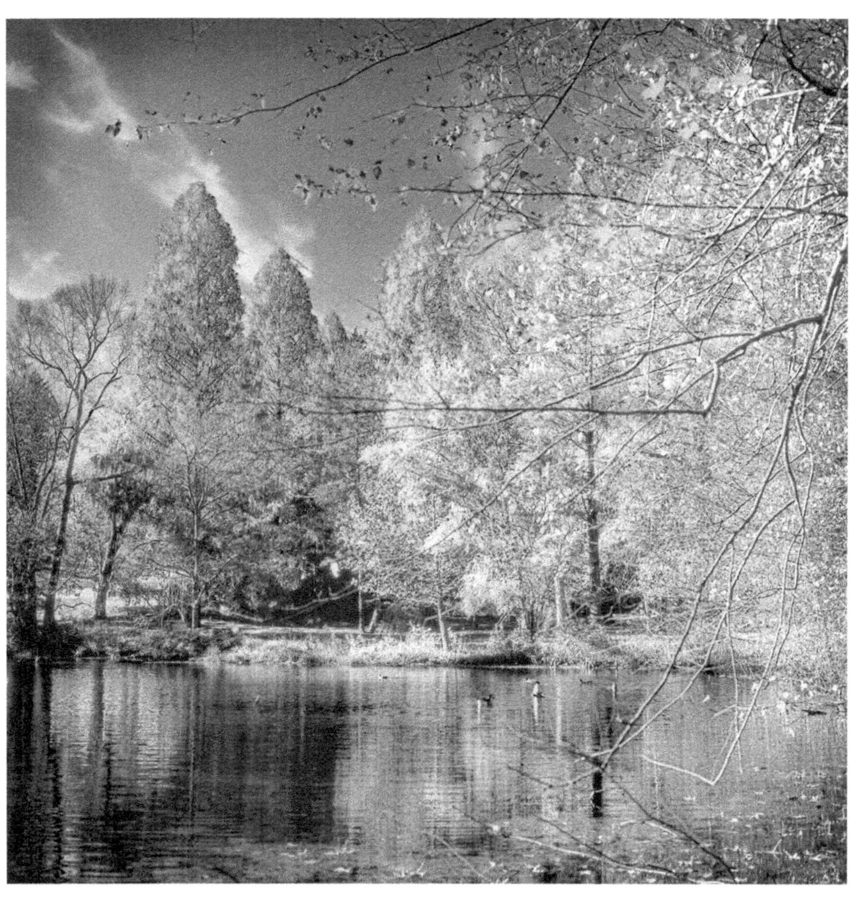

SUMMER

in the grass prairie
clouds quickly drifting over
lonely autumn tree

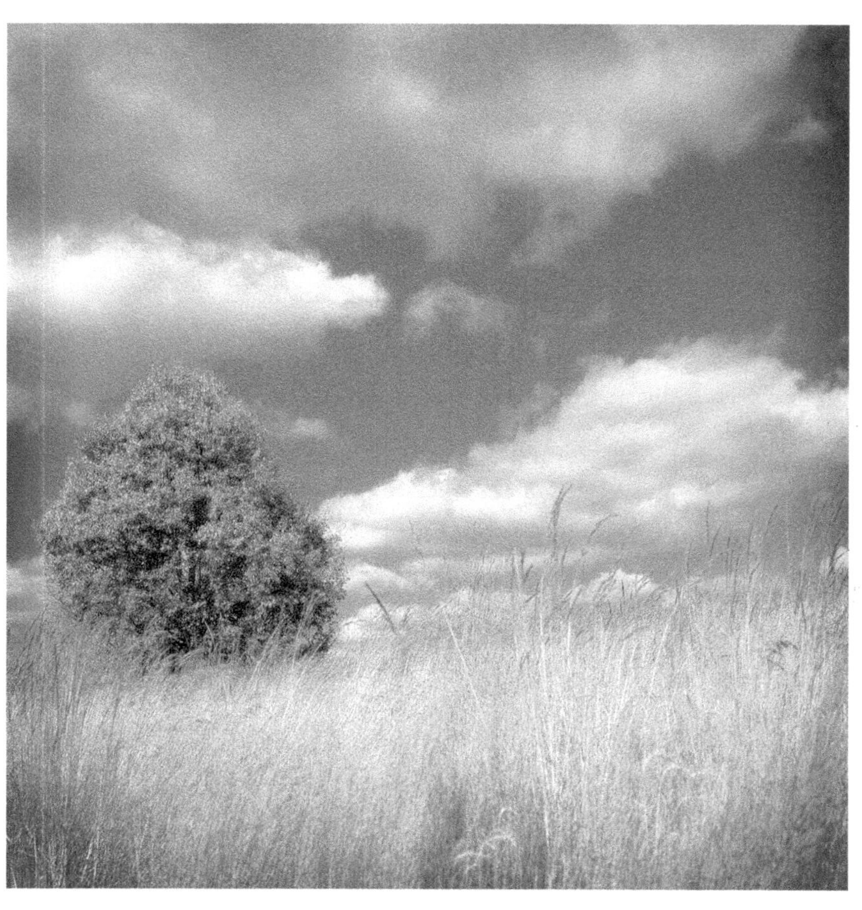

SNOW

in the window view
winter loads crack branches
—I feel lonely now

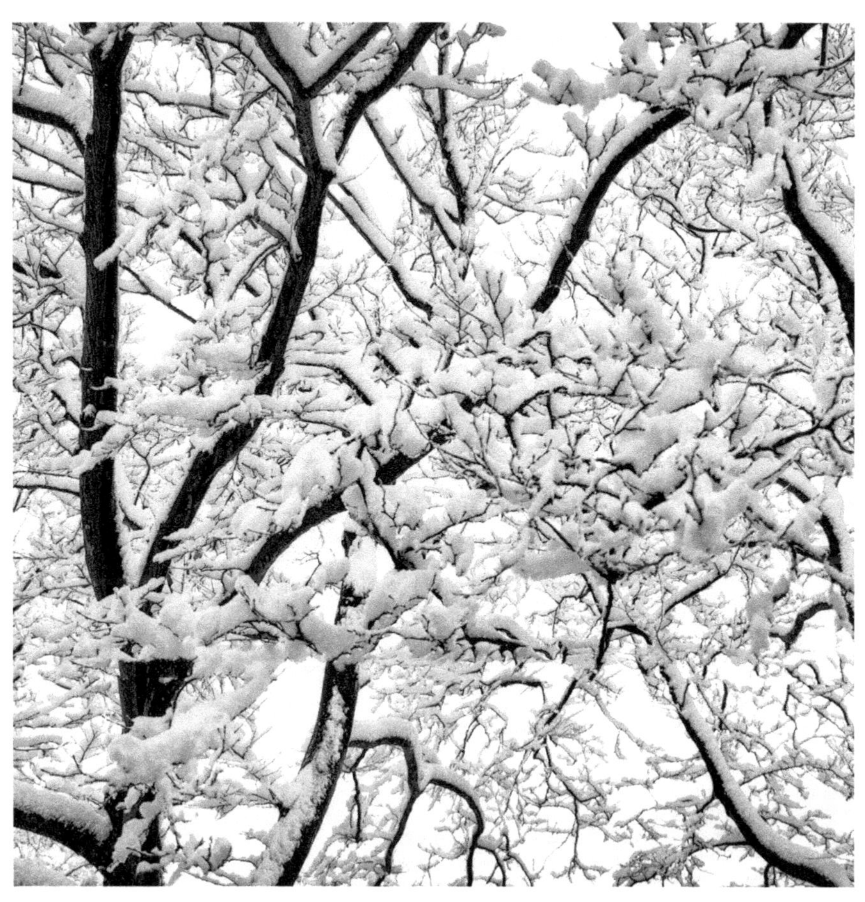

STREAM

in the forest green
loud stream runs over rocks
at the autumn view

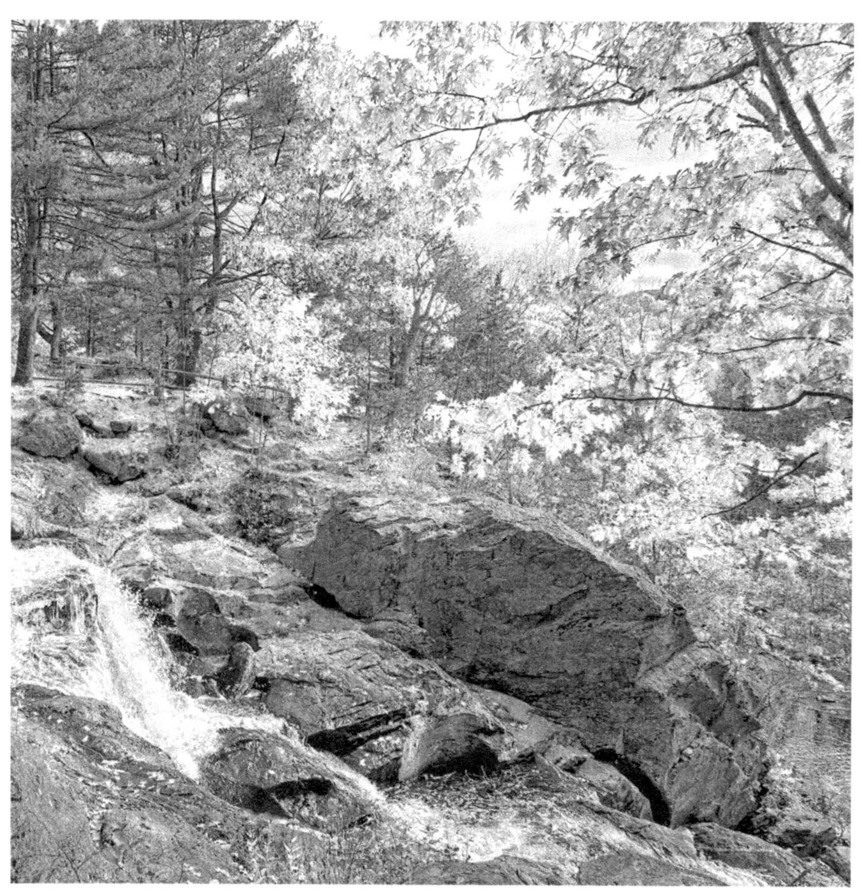

BUBBLES

in the deep lake
I hear the quiet of the sound—
early morning sun

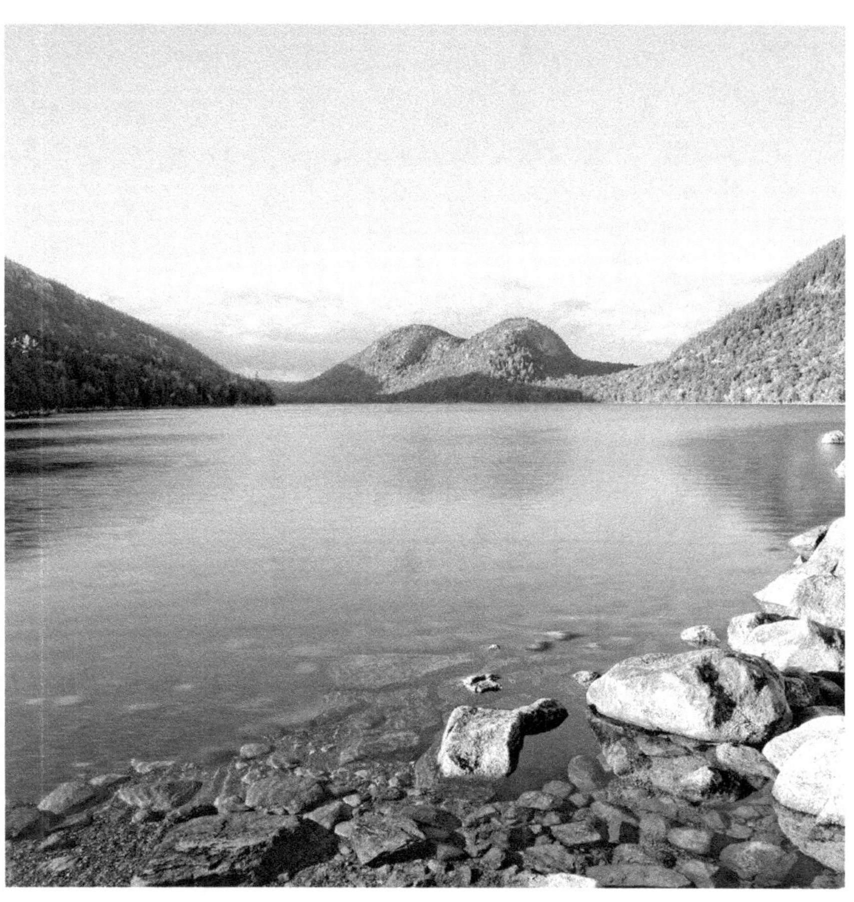

PIAZZALE

majestic city
tourists admiring the scene
sunset closing in

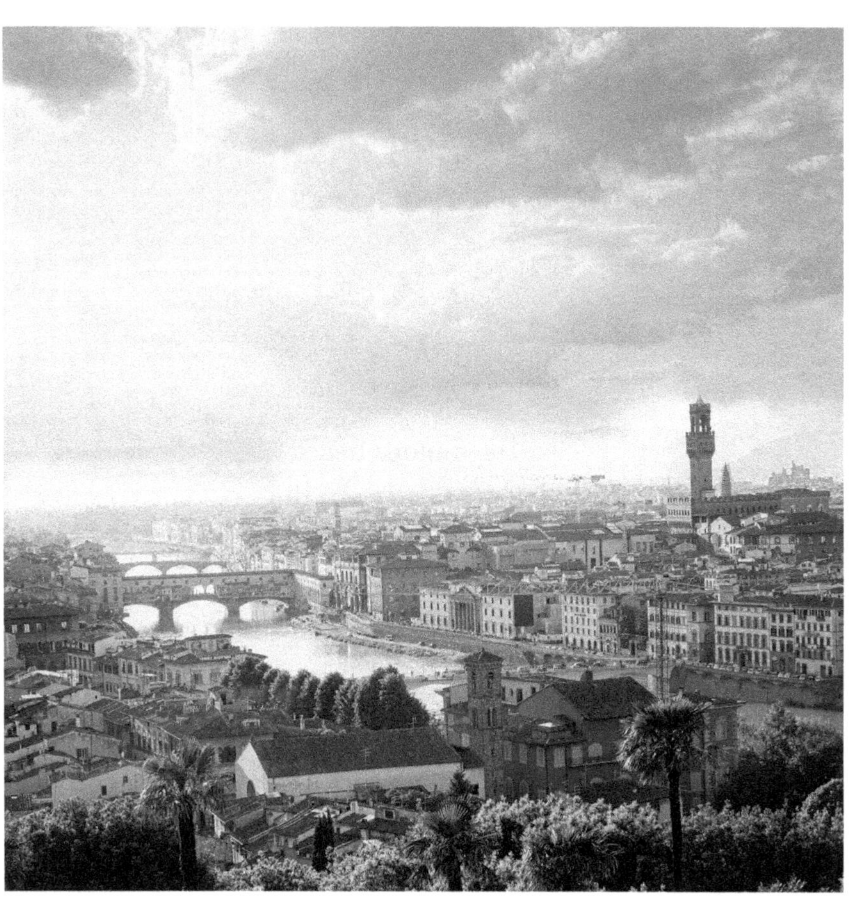

BEACH

at the famous beach
chalk cliffs slowly eroding—
haze is in the air

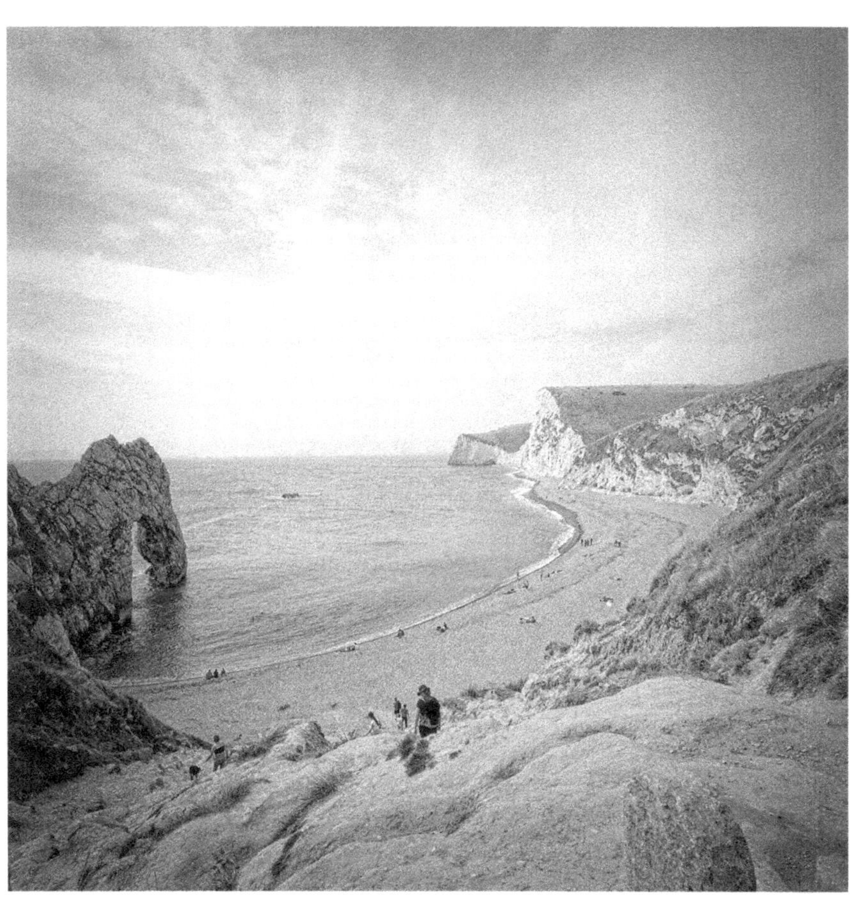

ETRETAT

on the famous coast
nature sentinels rise high—
midday beach stroll

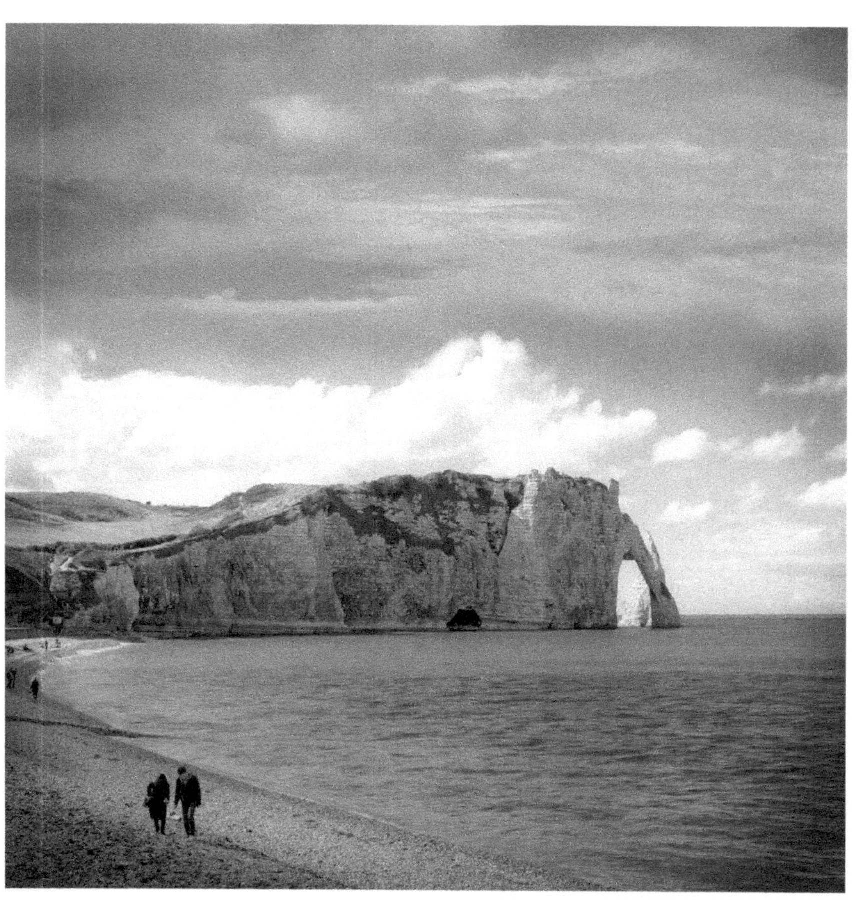

PATCH

on earth below
moving patch of light
evening approaches

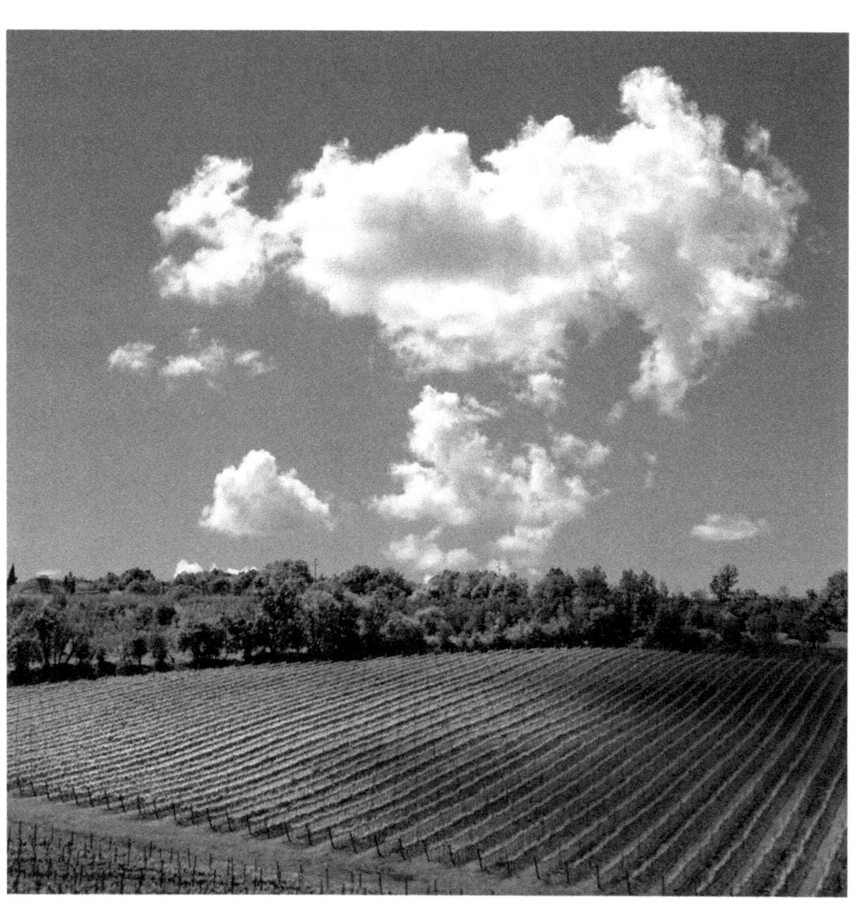

DUNES

ah...danish dunes
fresh country air
a voyage last year

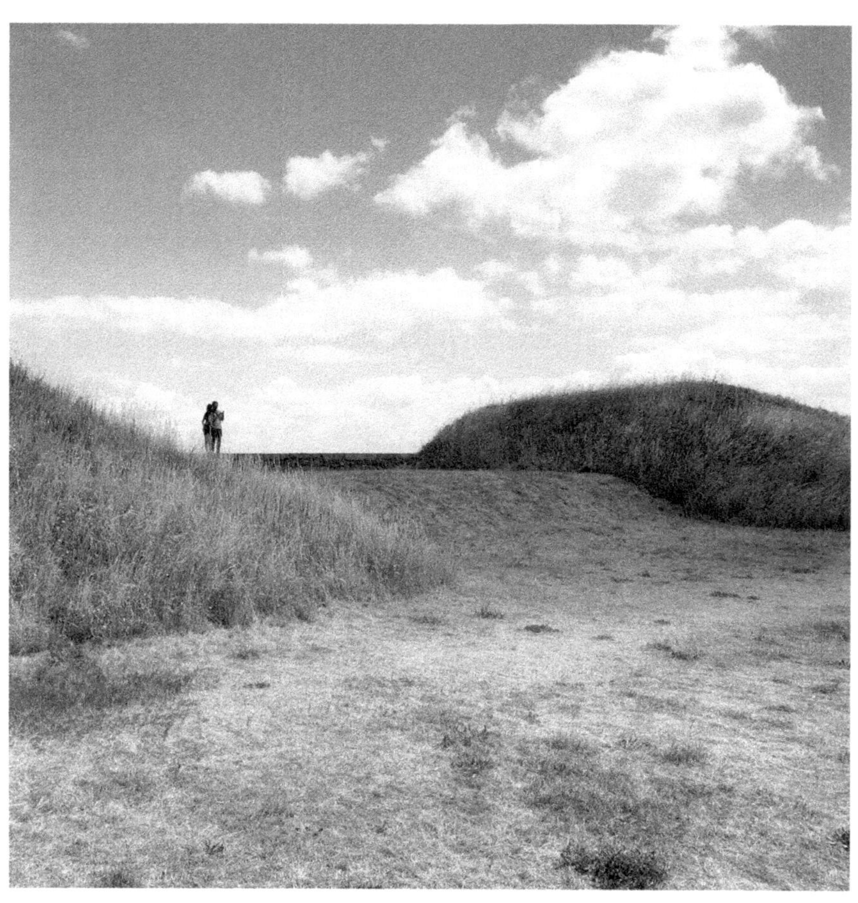

BAY

at an irish bay
calm water
imminent cloud bursting

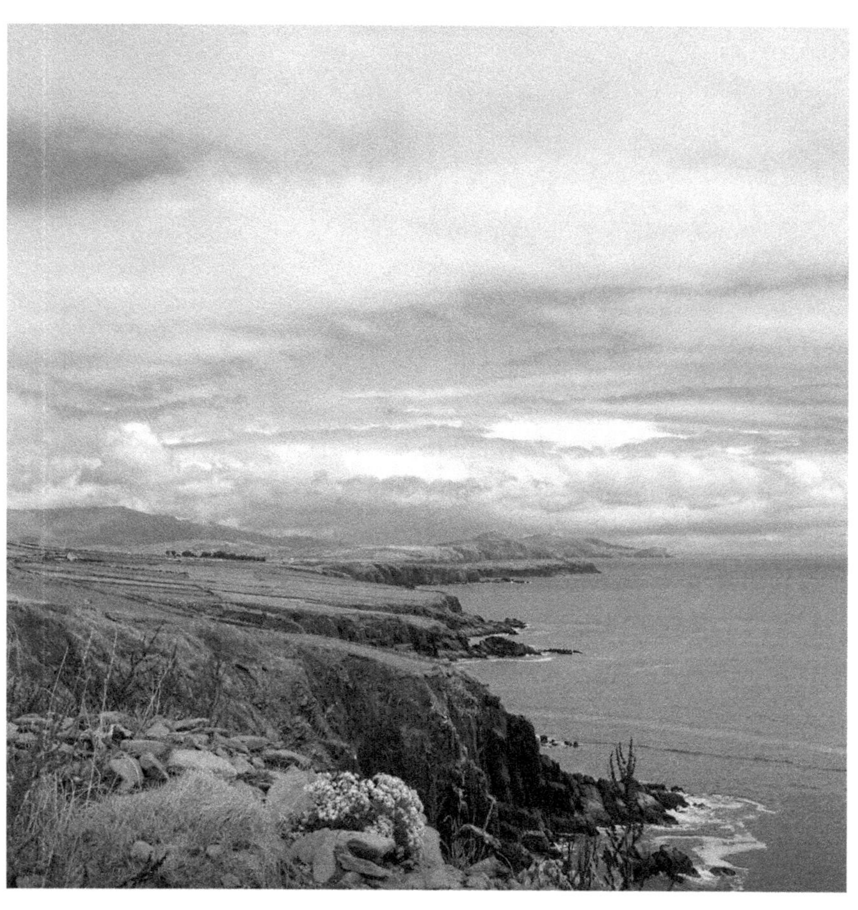

LETCHWORTH

leafage in the park
rain has stopped
autumn view

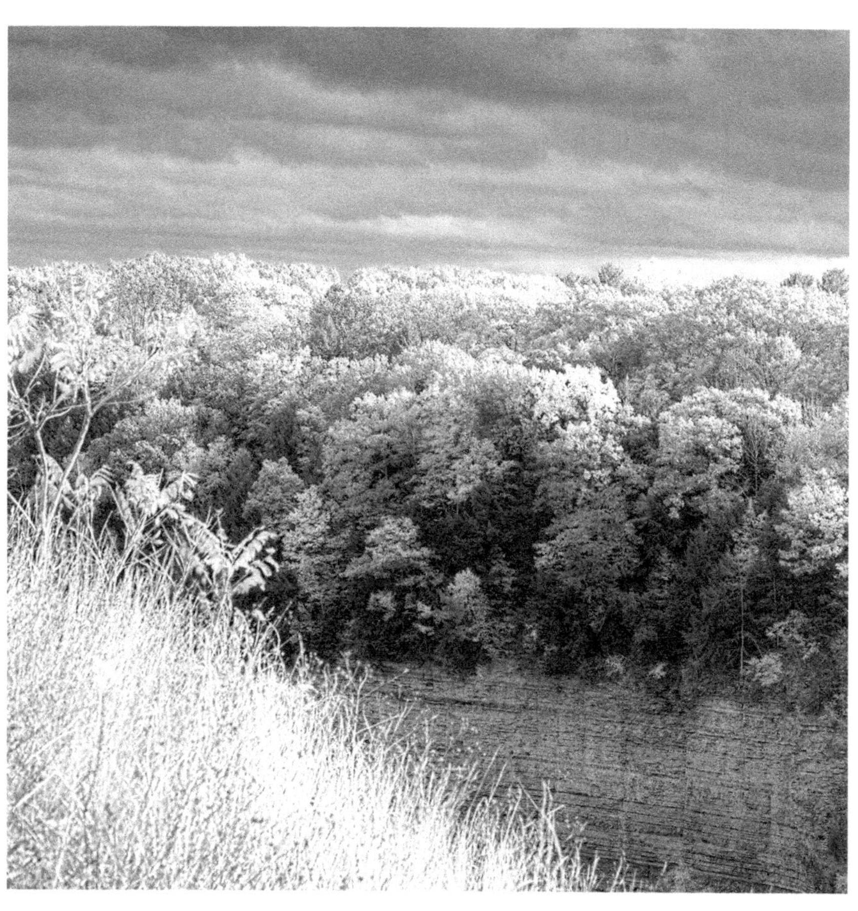

TULIPS

dutch country marvel
tulips blossom
early spring

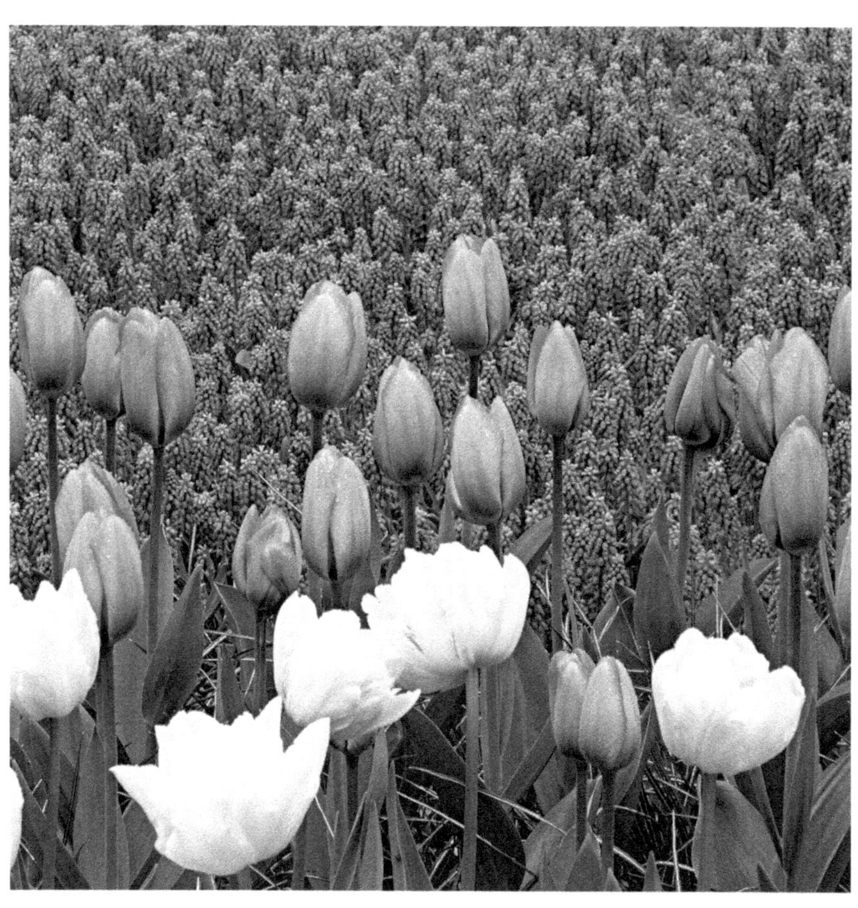

WHEEL

in the tuscan hills
a wheel is resting in peace
midday wine tasting

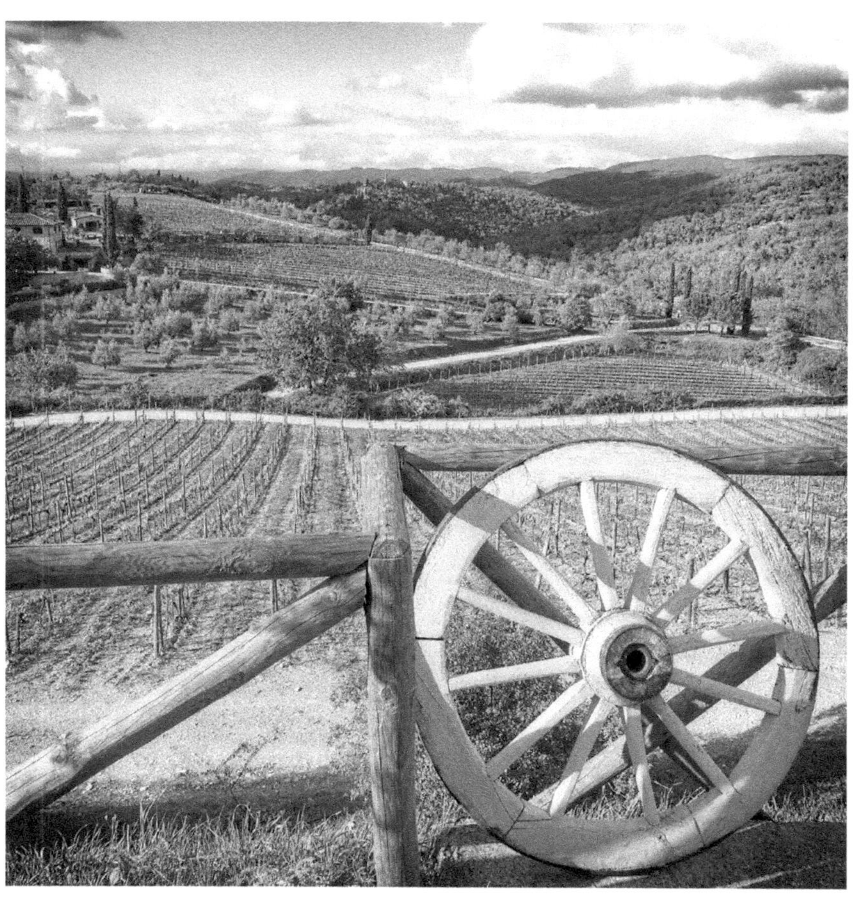

CLIFF

on the white chalk cliffs
people walking to the top
—magnificent view

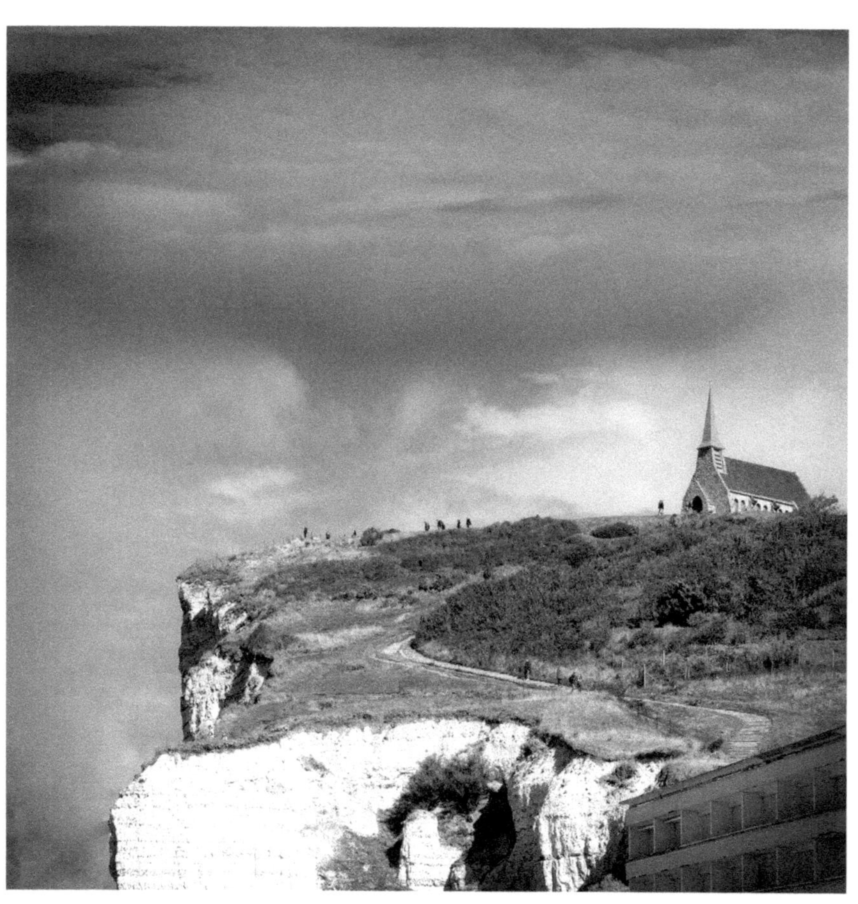

OCEAN

infinite ocean
forceful waves
—timeless motion

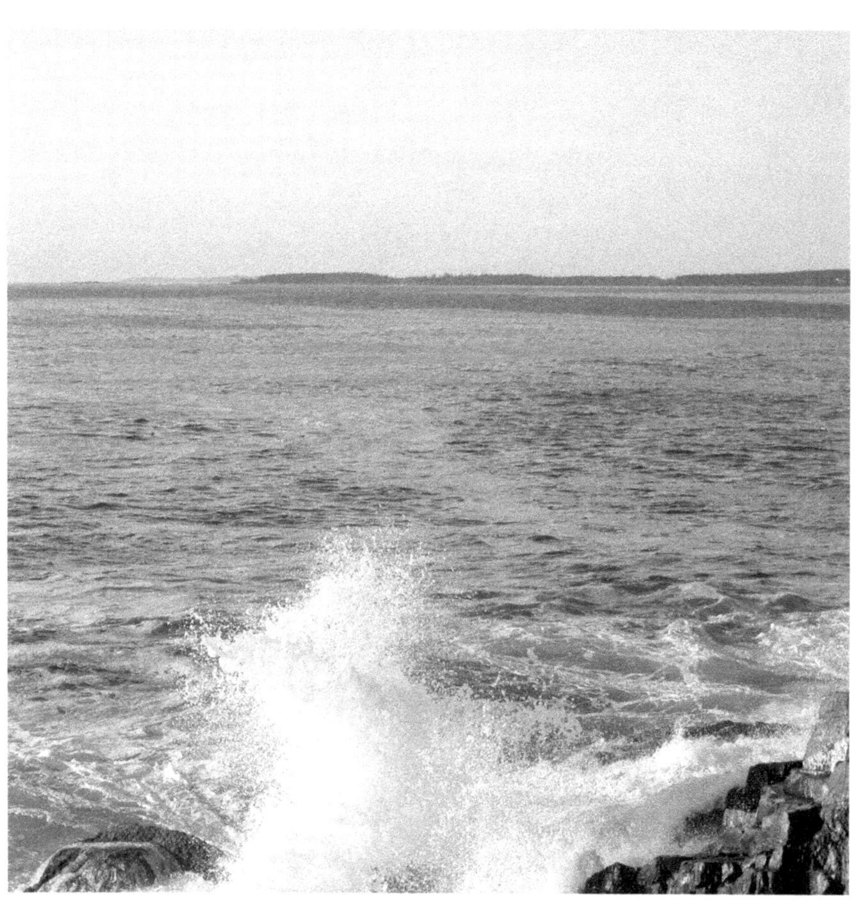

JULY

sand beach burns
boulders viewing big waves
—july scorching sun

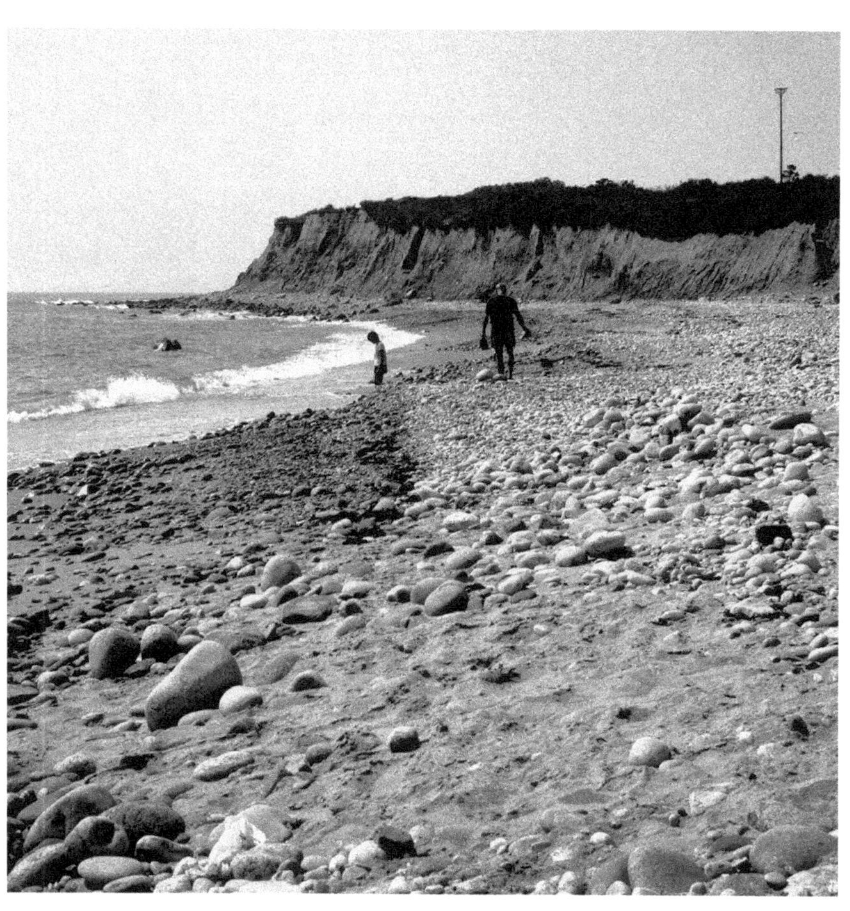

MOUNTAIN

at the famed abbey
early risers walk around
—high tide soon

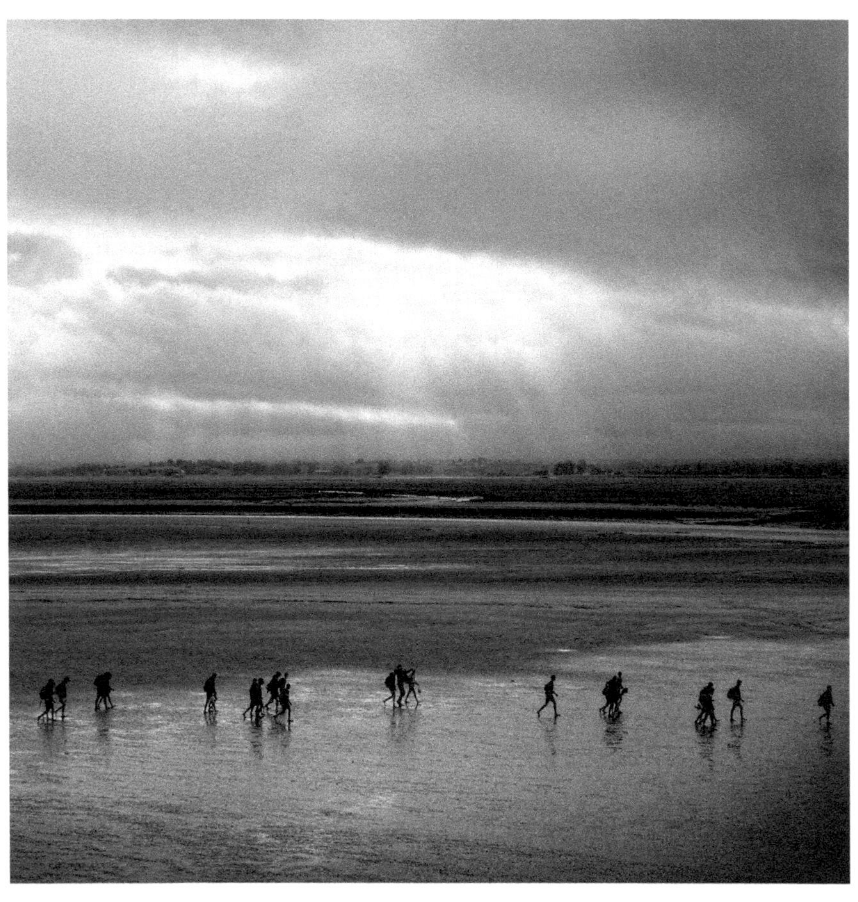

HORIZON

far horizon
too dark to continue
—imminent evening

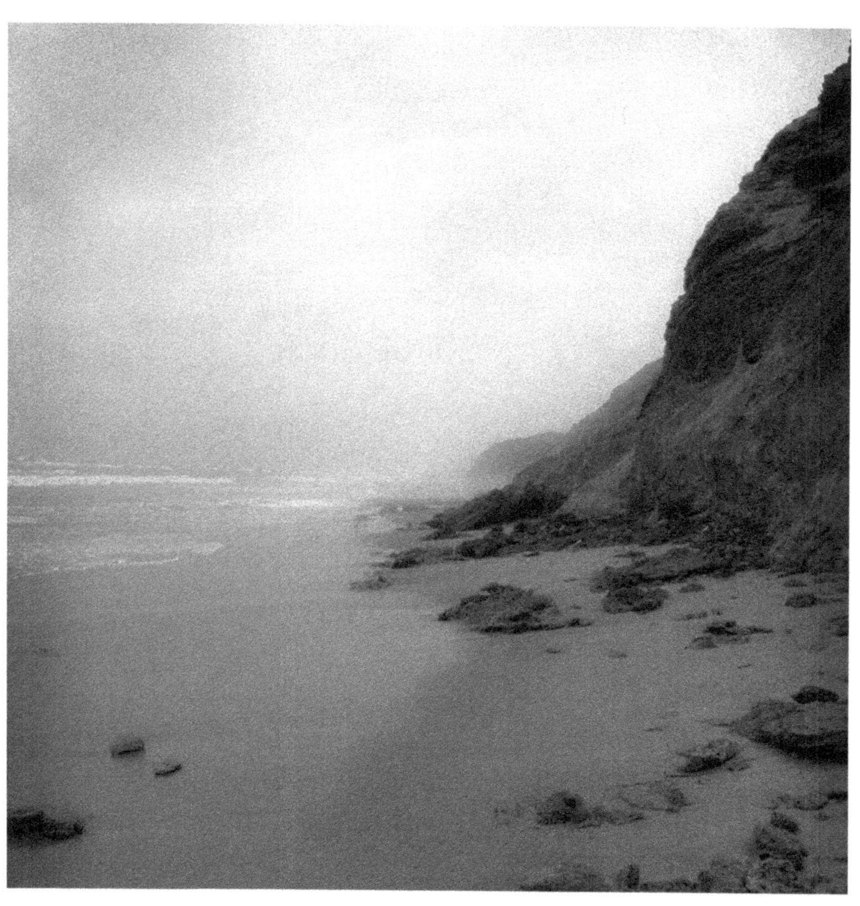

GORGE

in the rocky gorge
water falling loud
—morning fog smell

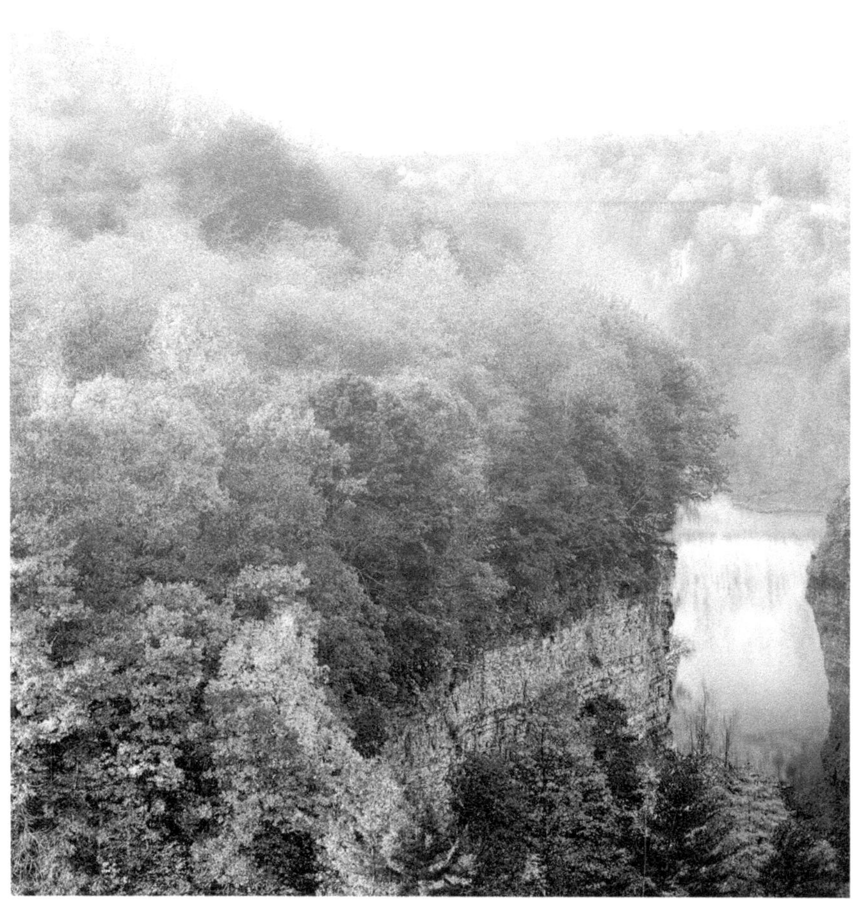

CALMNESS

primordial dawn
in the morning hour
—when light comes in

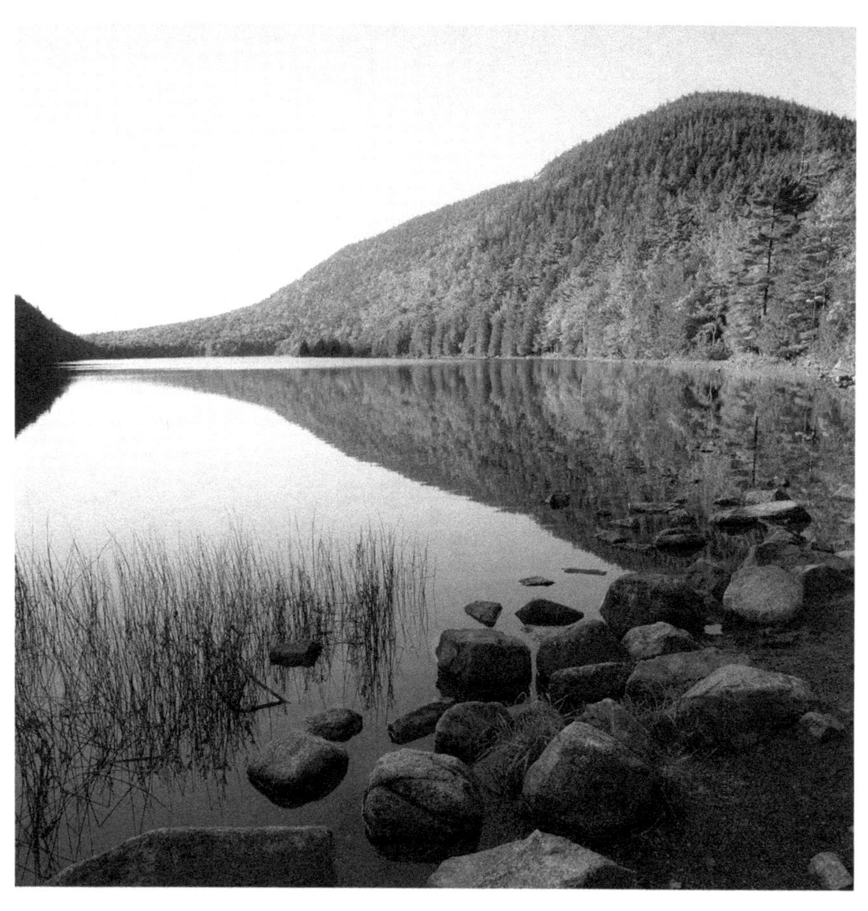

WAVE

over the city
time is passing
—menacing sea wave flies

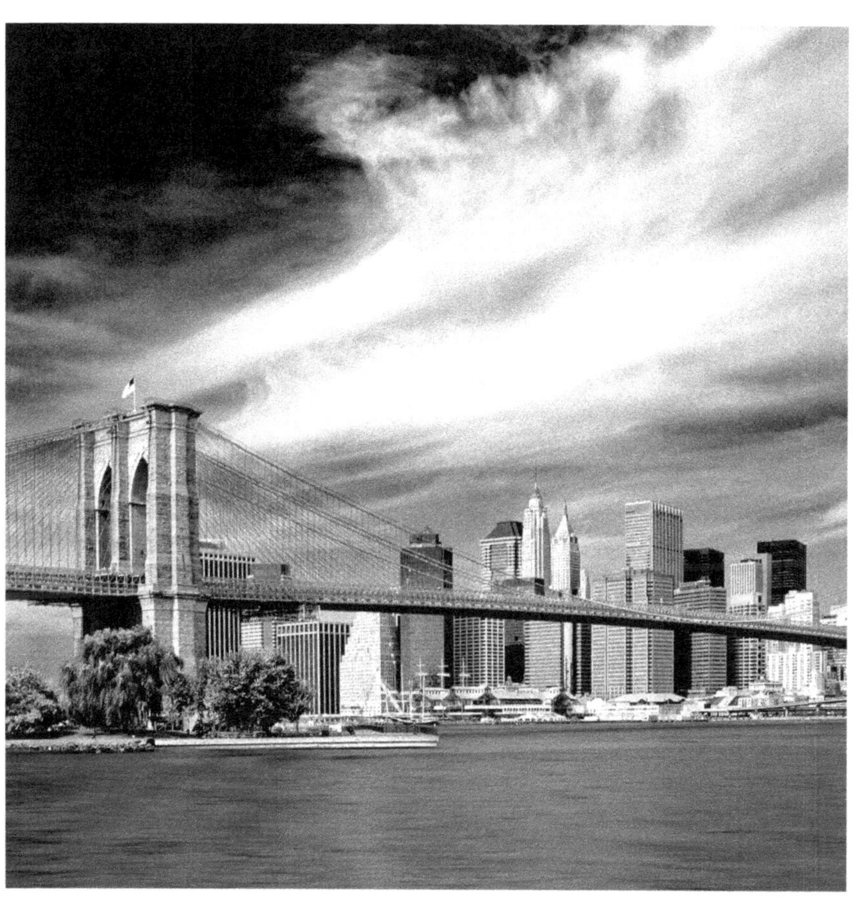

SOUNION

cape sounion I see
at the magical sunset
—when lovers delight

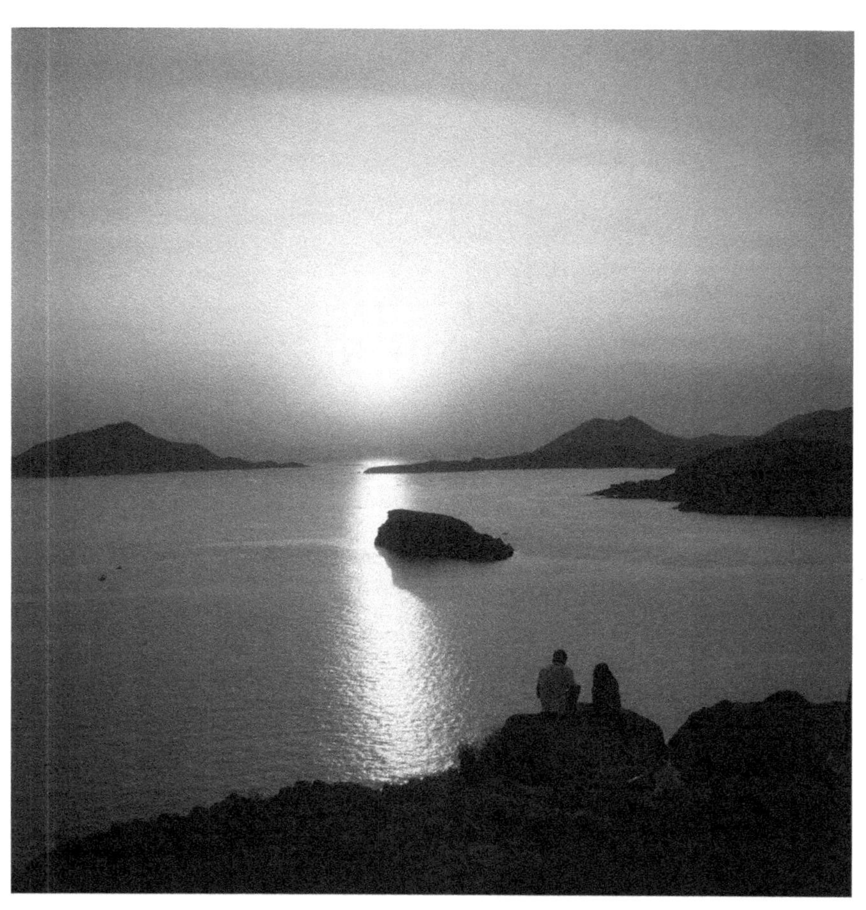

SANTORINI

on the rising hill
infinite blue space below
scorching midday sun

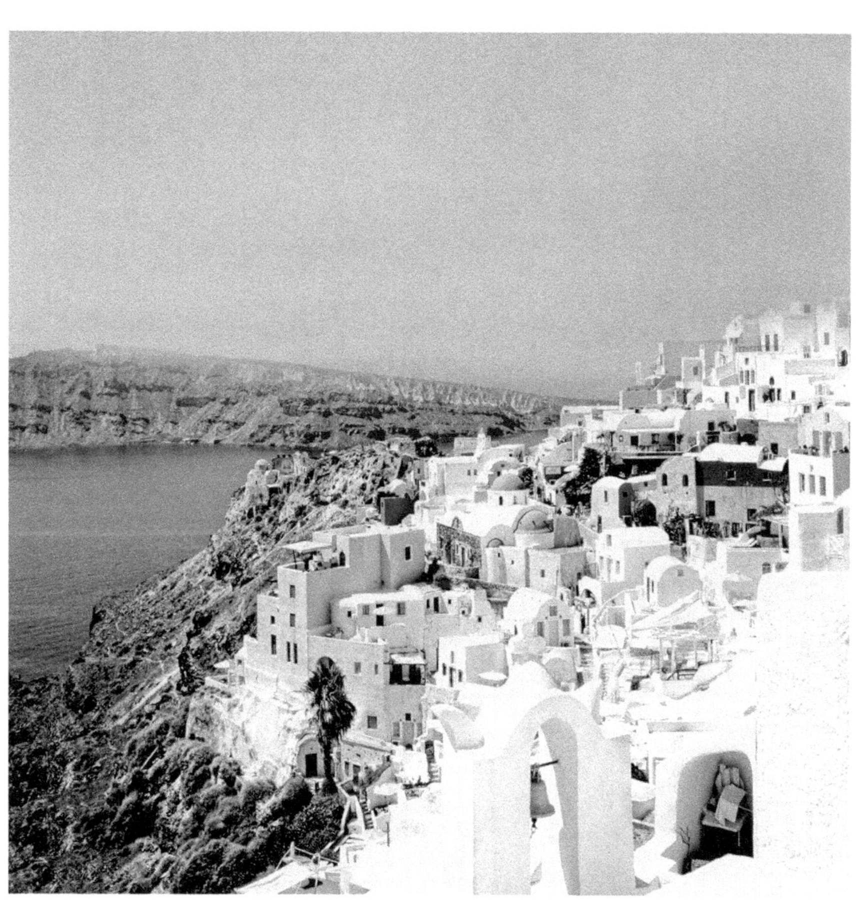

LAMP

up above
a sole lamp lights the sky
it is raining now

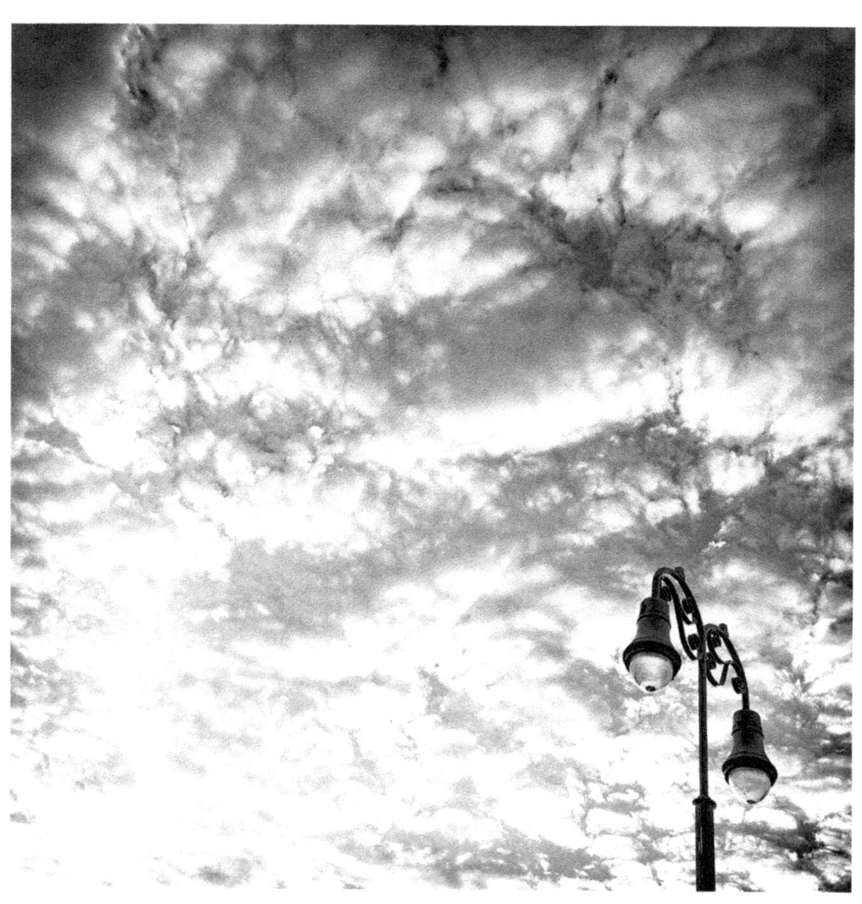

CONTOUR

a storm dances above
as night clouds push down the isle
—will I see morning

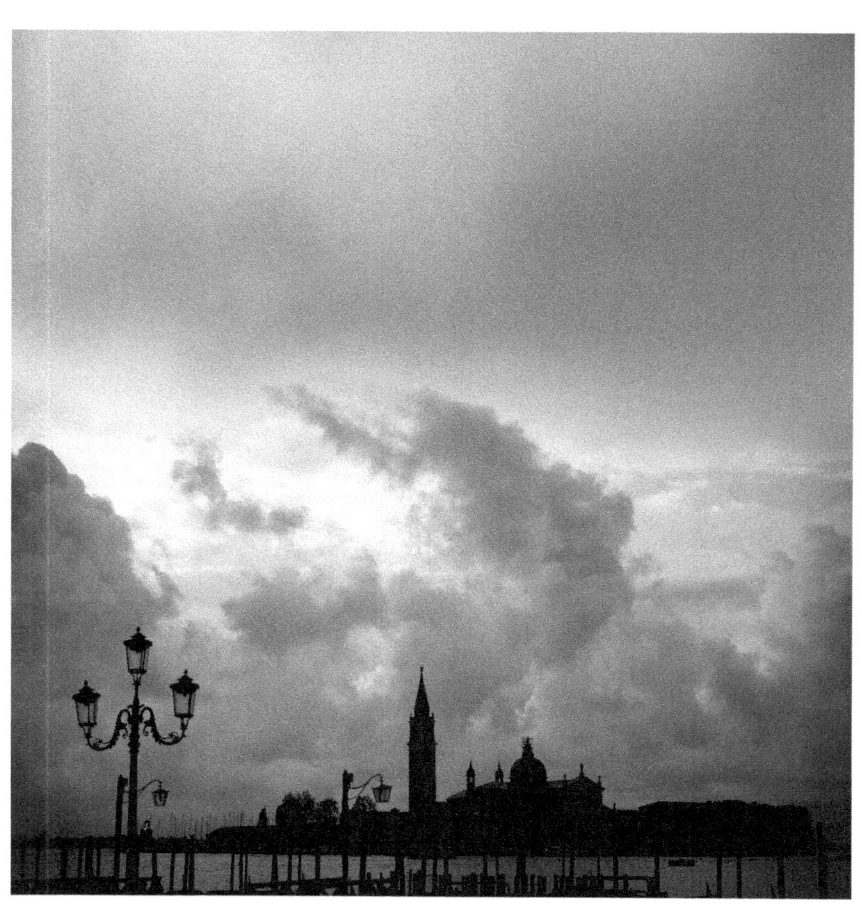

PORT

on zattere boardwalk
sun rays smiling through on folks
in late afternoon

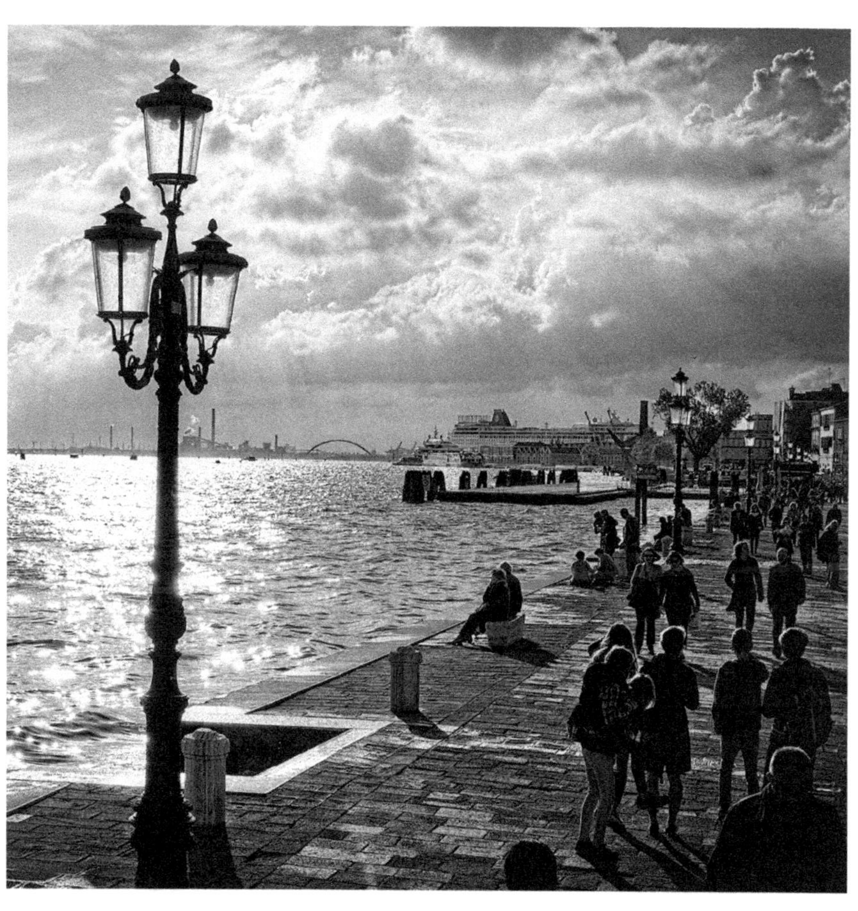

WATER

on the nordic sea
infinite view is soothing
observing at noon

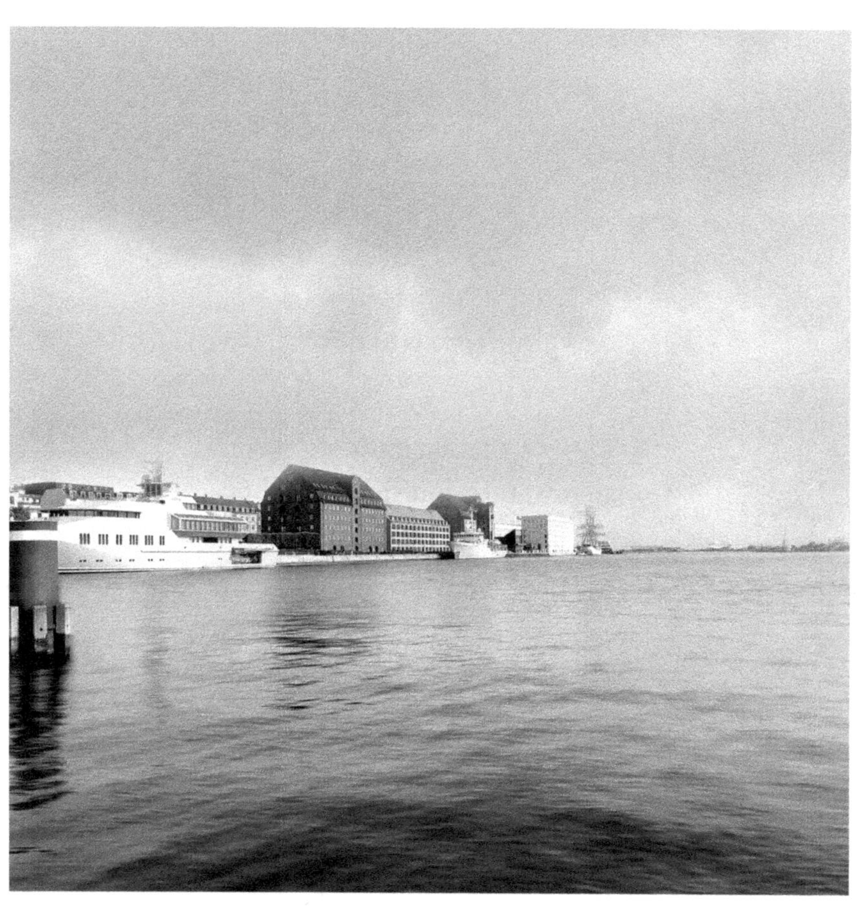

EVENING

at the sea outlook
calm waters and sleepy yachts
evening upon me

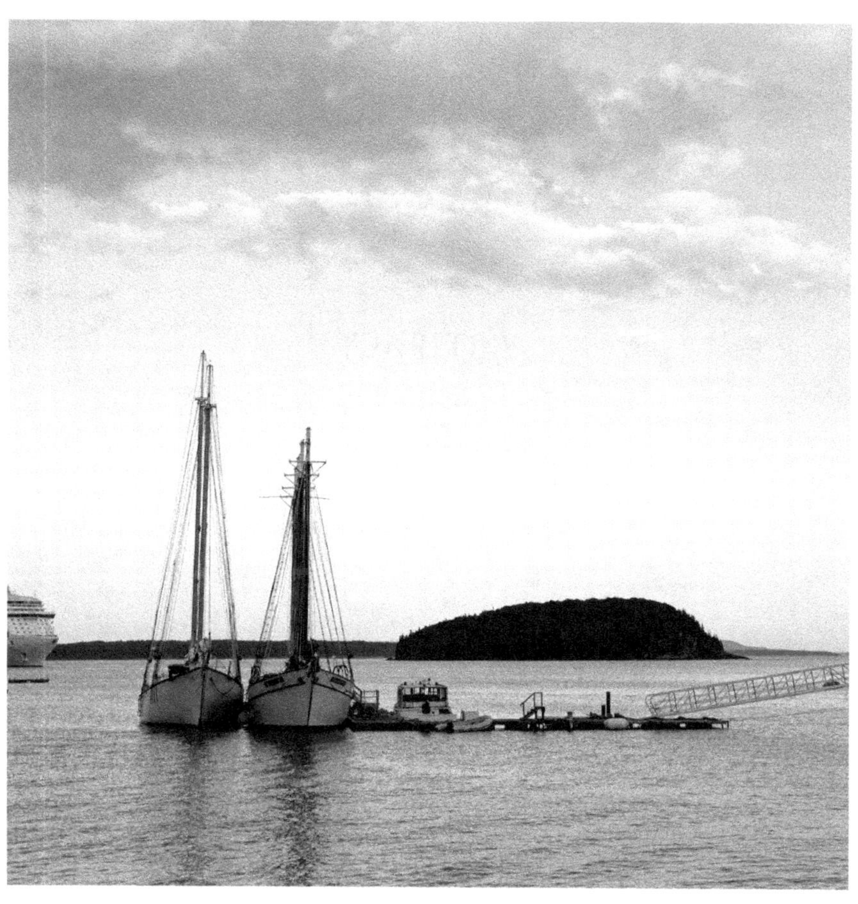

ARTIFACT

in the back garden
succumbed to human folly
—they kill old trees too

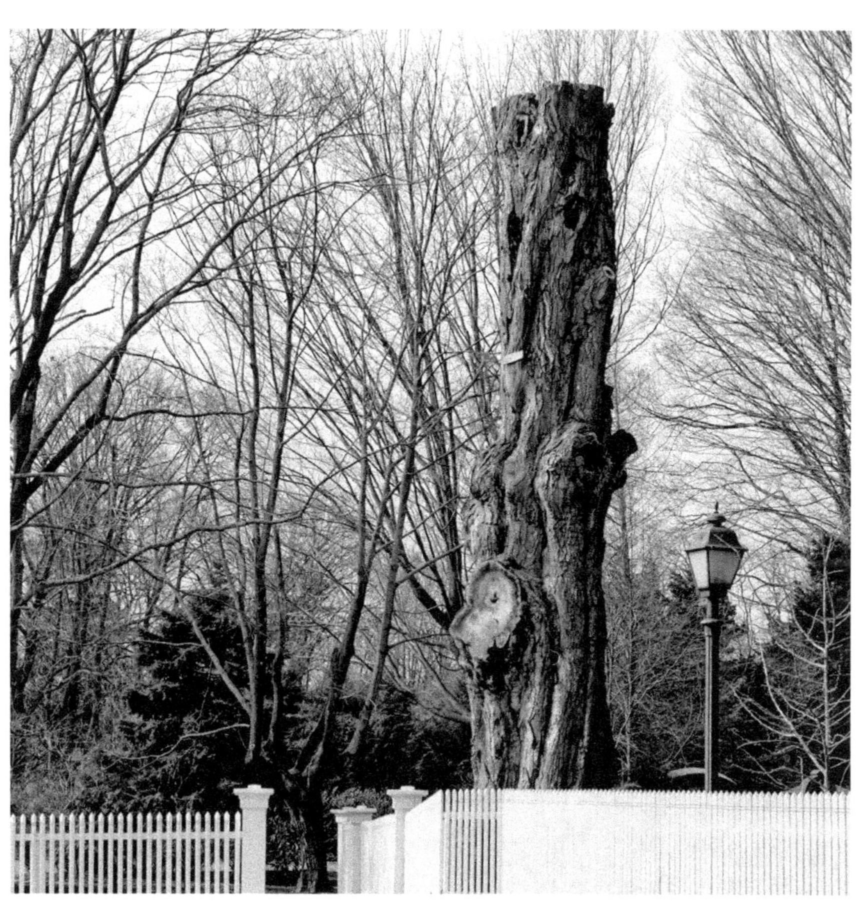

DANCE

in middle ocean
boats are dancing the tango
—I am dreaming now

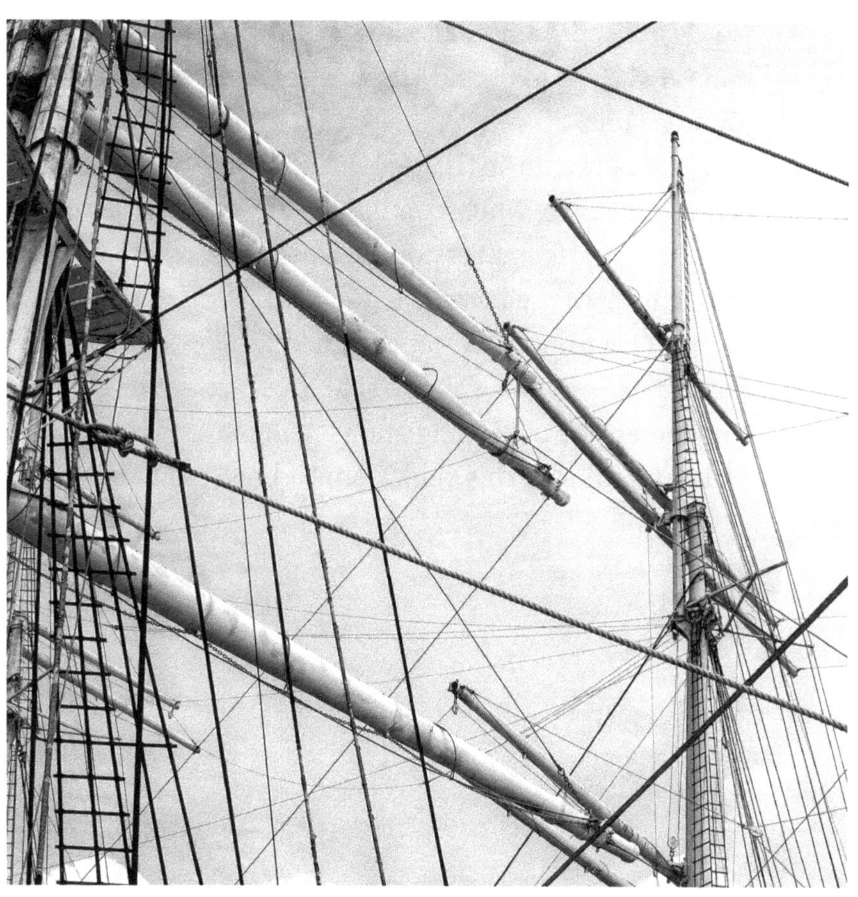

AFTERWORD

This book is a collection of words and images. The words are represented by the short form poetry of the Japanese style haiku, and the images are represented by photographs.

These two artistic forms can live without each other, however, when combined they become a unified form of artistic expression in which the whole is more powerful than the parts.

This print book was designed to show both of these artistic expressions side by side, in an effort to create a single message of reading and viewing. It is my hope that you have enjoyed this book's photo-haiku collection.

PROJECT NOTES

> The material in this book is a combination of two separate artistic processes, photography and poetry. The photographs were captured first and the haiku was added later. While some of the photographs were captured long ago, I wrote the companion haiku in 2025.

> In accordance with Japanese tradition, the thematic subject of the photo-haiku in this book is nature with a major concentration on landscape photography.

> Authors working with text (writers) and images (visual artists) that are skilled in both art forms, must decide how to arrange the combined content on a book's page. Text (in this case the haiku) could be imposed on the image (a most prevalent form of advertising), or it could be adjacent to the image.

> I respect photography and poetry as two separate forms of artistic expression. In this book, neither one encroaches on the physical space of the other. Although the haiku was written as an adjunct to the original photographs, my intent was to create one unified artistic expression.

> For the most part, the haiku were written by following the traditional Japanese criteria (5-7-5) for a total of 17 syllables, but I have also deviated from the Japanese

rule, sometimes quite substantially in the French and Italian haiku.

> Extensive efforts and deep diving into memory were necessary to recreate the moment of the click for the purpose of writing the haiku. Past memory associations inspired by photographs, assisted in the writing.

> It is a valid process to capture photographs, for which haiku would be written years later to clarify, enhance or create new meaning with 5-7-5 syllables.

REFERENCES

Kenneth Yasuda, *The Japanese Haiku,* Charles E. Tuttle Company 1957.

Blyth R. H. , *Haiku Vol. II Spring*, The Hokuseido Press, Heian International 1981.

Haas Robert, *The Essential Haiku versions of Basho, Buson, and Issa*, The Ecco Press 1994.

Reichold Jane, *Basho The complete Haiku*, Kodansha USA Inc. 2008.

J. Higginson William with Penny Harter, *The haiku handbook*, Kodansha International 1989.

Cummings Alan, *Haiku Love*, The Overlook Press, New York 2013.

Photographs of imagined Haiku Landscape, Misumura Suiko

Shoin Publishing Co., Ltd 2018, Japan nature scenery Photograph Association.
Judith Patt, Michiko Warkentyne, Barry Till, *Haiku Japanese Art and Poetry*, Pomegranate Communications, Inc. 2010.
Sylvia Forges-Ryan, Edward Ryan, *Take a Deep Breath*, Kodansha International 2002.

AUTHOR BIOGRAPHY

Daniel Heller RA is a professional architect visual artist and publisher of visual literature books. He lives and works in New York.

The author expresses himself in figurative and abstract artworks in a variety of media. His photographic portfolio includes for the most part, landscapes, architectural subjects and urban scenes. He writes illustrates and publishes visual literature fine art and photography books and is the author illustrator of the book '*Plato's Visual Utopia*'.

His artistic expression writing and illustration style, is mostly representational realistic, depicting subject matter that was strongly influenced by the surrealists. He exhibited in several countries and his works are held in private collections in Australia, the UK, Israel, and the United States.

The author graduated with a Bachelor's degree from the school of architecture in Florence and has practiced architecture for over 40 years, designing numerous healing environments in the United States.

READER'S NOTES:

www.ingramcontent.com/pod-product-compliance
Lightning Source LLC
LaVergne TN
LVHW010932110826
845149LV00013B/2567

* 9 7 9 8 9 9 9 0 3 7 1 0 7 *